CW00740207

flowers for elizabeth

A Collection of Elizabethan Inspired Motifs

Susan O'Connor

INSPIRATIONS

Welcome

The embroidery of the Elizabethan period (1558–1603) is characterised by both its style and subject matter. Especially beautiful are the wonderfully sinuous scrolling designs encapsulating the plants and flowers that were so popular at this time. Sweet honeysuckle, primrose, columbine, gillyflower and heartsease are only a few of the flowers lavishly used to embellish clothing and household furnishings, bringing the newly discovered delights of the garden into the home. Four centuries later these wonderful motifs have lost none of their appeal.

Take a leisurely stroll through a 16th century garden while stitching these delightful flowers and fruits. Inspired by the embroidery of Elizabethan England, choose from twenty-nine colourful designs to stitch a superb throw with wool threads or a selection of elegant needlework accessories using lustrous silk.

Superb photography, detailed instruction and step-by-step stitch diagrams make this a beautiful addition to the needleworker's bookcase.

Contents

The Elizabethans

The embroidery of the Elizabethan era has been the subject of endless fascination and inspiration to generations of embroiderers and those interested in the decorative arts. Most needleworkers in the western world would be familiar with the distinctive embroidery of the 16th century. Numerous books have been written, stitches and techniques explored and dissected, embroideries reworked and designs reinterpreted. So why does this particular period in history offer such a rich needlework legacy and who was the woman after whom it was named?

YOUNG ELIZABETH

Elizabeth was born on September 7, 1533, the daughter of Henry VIII and Anne Boleyn, his second wife. She was the second surviving child of Henry as he had also fathered a daughter, Mary, with his first wife, Katherine of Aragon. Arguably England's most famous king, Henry married six times and had numerous other relationships. Of his marriages, four were annulled, one wife died and one survived him as Queen consort. At his death in 1547, he was survived by only three children, Mary, Elizabeth and nine year old Edward, son of Jane Seymour, his third wife.

Upon Henry's marriage to Jane, Elizabeth was declared illegitimate and removed from the line of succession, just as her half-sister Mary had been when Henry married Anne Boleyn.

Elizabeth was no longer a princess and she was given into the care of a governess. Under the guidance of a succession of tutors, Elizabeth undertook extensive studies and by the end of her formal education in 1550, she was the best educated woman of her generation.

This was a valuable asset as after her father's death, her half-brother became King Edward VI. Only nine years old, Edward was too young and the country was ruled by a Regency Council until he came of age. Edward died at fifteen, his will excluding both Mary and Elizabeth from the line of succession and naming his cousin, Lady Jane Grey as his heir. The English people rose in protest over this and Jane lasted only nine days as queen before Mary was reinstated and became Mary I on July 19, 1553.

Above: Henry VIII and Elizabeth I as princess c1546

Mary's reign did not last long and on November 17, 1558, she died childless, leaving the throne to her half-sister Elizabeth.

Elizabeth I, Queen of England and Queen of Ireland, was crowned at Westminster Abbey on January 15, 1559 at the age of twenty-five.

It would seem that amongst all the marriages, annulments, executions etc. that there was little love amongst Henry's offspring, but much of the apparent acrimony was caused by religion and the tumultuous state of the church at the time.

When Henry VIII became King of England, it was a Catholic country under the auspices of the Pope in Rome. Marriages were arranged with a view to form alliances between countries that shared religious beliefs. Spain and France were both Catholic countries and potential threats to England. Henry's marriage to Katherine, a Spanish princess, created an alliance between England and Spain. When he wished to have his marriage to Katherine annulled and marry Anne Boleyn, the Pope refused and Henry was forced to break from the Roman Catholic Church, placing himself as head of the Catholic Church of England. At the same time, the Protestant Reformation was occurring, initially as an attempt to reform the corrupt Roman Catholic Church but eventually leading to the formation of the Protestant Churches.

Edward VI was a Protestant and under his reign, the Church of England became Protestant, abolishing clerical celibacy and the mass, ensuring that services were performed in English, not Latin. Mary, in turn, was a Catholic and despite her half-brother's attempts to keep her from the throne, she proceeded to undo many of his Protestant reforms, attempting to return England to the Catholic Church. Known as 'Bloody Mary', she was responsible for the execution of more than

three hundred religious dissenters, having them burned at the stake. Elizabeth was lucky to have survived Mary's reign as she was seen by many in the Catholic Church as a threat to the queen.

Elizabeth had been raised as a Protestant, so under her long reign, the Protestant Church of England was reinstated and became firmly established. The only remaining Catholic thorn was the daughter of Elizabeth's cousin James, Mary, Queen of Scots.

ELIZABETH AS QUEEN

Under Elizabeth I, England enjoyed a long period of prosperity and relative peace. Trade and exploration flourished and the period 1558-1603 is widely regarded as a golden age in English history, a time of great discovery and enlightenment.

With the general growth of material comfort in the reign of Elizabeth, domestic embroidery flourished. It is interesting to note that, prior to this

Above: Elizabeth I, 1590. Costume elaborately embroidered with blackwork.

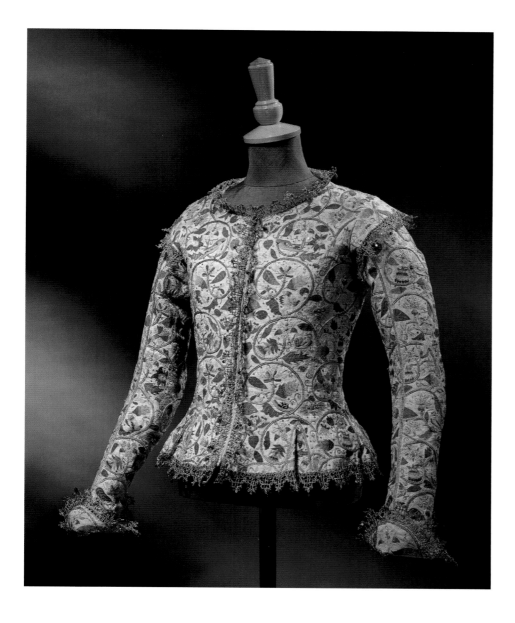

stomachers, caps, breeches, capes, gloves, coifs and smocks; clothing for both men and women. Two main colour schemes were employed for both furnishing and costume embroidery; monochrome or single colour embroidery, usually black onto a white or natural background, and polychrome or multi-coloured embroidery.

Blackwork, or 'Spanish' embroidery was made popular in England by Katherine of Aragon, Henry VIII's first wife, but this style of embroidery was known there before her arrival.

Unlike the somewhat stiff, uninspiring counted thread work that is done today, Elizabethan blackwork designs were a combination of free-flowing surface embroidery and counted thread filling stitches. Some pieces contained no counted thread work at all, instead using 'speckling' or 'seeding' to create interest.

Often used on smocks, coifs and sleeves, the severe palette of blackwork contrasted beautifully with the richly coloured embroidery that was used to decorate other parts of a costume. With the addition of gold and silver threads, a liberal sprinkling of spangles, an intricate lace ruff and large amounts of jewellery, the affluent, well dressed Elizabethan was a spectacular sight, regardless of gender.

The decorative motifs that were used were primarily floral with the addition of numerous animals, birds and insects. Designs varied from formalised geometric arrangements with decorative strapping to loose, free flowing patterns filled with realistic representations of flowers and fruit.

One of the most predominant and easily recognised styles is that of an overall pattern of sinuous floral scrolls, filled with an exuberant display of favourite Elizabethan flowers: gillyflower, heartsease, primrose, columbine, honeysuckle, cinquefoil, eglantine, buttercup, rose and daisy. Interest was

period, little material evidence remains of any English domestic embroidery. During the 13th and 14th centuries, England was renowned for the magnificent ecclesiastical embroidery, Opus Anglicanum, that it produced but little is known of textiles for the home and personal use. With changes in the church and the dissolution of monasteries, the importation of silk from the orient and manufacture of steel needles, plus the greatly improved economic position of the middle class,

domestic embroidery came into its own. Through pieces of stitching still in existence and portraits of the time, it is easy to see the important role that embroidery played.

Elizabethan embroidery can be divided into two main groups; furnishing embroideries and costume embroideries. In the first group are table and floor carpets, cushions, bed hangings, pillow covers and large bed covers.

Costume embroideries include bodices, jackets, petticoats, bags,

Above: Margaret Layton's linen jacket embroidered with richly coloured silk, silver and silver gilt thread. England, c1610. © V&A images, Victoria and Albert Museum.

not limited only to what grew naturally in England. Pomegranate, tulip, pineapple and peony also found their place in the Elizabethan bouquet. Add the snails, butterflies, birds, caterpillars and dragonflies naturally associated with plants, one could be forgiven for thinking that such glorious delights were newly discovered.

THE ELIZABETHAN GARDEN

Growing flowers, herbs and fruit purely for pleasure was a new concept for the Elizabethans. Prior to this time, plants were grown within walled enclosures only for medicinal use or as food. Flowers were used as church decoration and for festivals and the garden was certainly not regarded as a place for pleasure and enjoyment. All this changed under Elizabeth's reign with the building of lavish country houses and the planting of the surrounding gardens, complete with all manner of fountains and follies. Elizabeth was fond of summer progresses into the country and her affluent courtiers were certainly eager to impress their Queen. Outdoor pleasures, games and dancing were favourite pursuits in fine weather and the finer the surroundings, the better. Wildflowers were brought from the hedgerows and fields to be cultivated as garden plants. Rare exotics came from far off lands,

some to thrive, others to fail miserably in the unfamiliar climate. Peacocks strutted along lavish garden walks, beneath arbours of perfumed roses and amongst branches laden with fruit. A fine garden was divided into compartments or garden rooms, each one uniquely designed and containing different plants. Knot gardens or parterres were popular and it is easy to see these ornate designs echoed in the embroidery of the time.

The Elizabethans revelled in the colours, sounds and fragrances of the garden and desired to capture this transient beauty on their furnishings and clothing.

Embroidery became a popular pastime for ladies who took their designs from illustrated flower books or florilegia and spent their leisure time stitching blossoms onto all manner of items. Whilst it was a pleasant way for ladies to while away the hours, embroidery was a highly regarded profession for men. Given the time hungry nature of needlework, it was prudent to have pieces professionally worked in one of the embroidery houses that existed at the time. The quality of professional work was also superior to that produced in the home and this was especially important when giving gifts of embroidery.

Bookbinding embroidered by Princess Elizabeth at age 11, 1544.

FLOWERS FOR ELIZABETH

By the beginning of Elizabeth's reign, it had become customary to present gifts to the monarch at the New Year. As her reign continued, it became well known that the Queen was a keen needlewoman and enjoyed gifts of beautiful embroidery, preferring them to the more traditional purses of gold pieces. Keeping favour with the Queen was extremely important and records show that her courtiers spared little expense to impress her with gifts of jewellery and exquisitely embroidered clothing. Many of these gifts were carefully planned, choosing motifs of flowers that Elizabeth was known to favour, such as the heartsease and eglantine. It was not unusual for clothing to be given before being made up so that her tailor could fit the garment properly and not have to unpick seams. Smaller items, such as coifs, stockings, gloves and sweet bags were popular gifts from lower ranked courtiers, servants and tradesmen. No matter how large or small the gift, it would be lavishly embroidered with flowers as the predominant motifs.

AN ELIZABETHAN LEGACY

Portraits from this period ably demonstrate the Elizabethan love of ornate floral decoration. Those pieces of stitching that remain in museums give us a rare insight into the colours, designs and techniques that were in common use.

Elizabeth died on March 24, 1603, just six months short of her 70th birthday. At a time when the average life expectancy was around 45 years, she had lived a long, full life. Although she never married or produced an heir, she left an unsurpassed legacy in the decorative arts, a sumptuous feast of glorious embroidery design that continues to be enjoyed today.

Francis Bacon, Of Gardens

Francis Bacon held that

"...in the royal ordering of gardens there ought to be gardens for all months of the year, in which severally things of beauty may then be in season..."

He then recommended these flowering plants and trees from those in season in each month.

<small>FRANCIS BACON, ON GARDENS, IN ESSAYS OR COUNSELS, CIVIL AND MORAL (1597)</small>

"These particulars are for the climate of London."

THE LATTER PART OF NOVEMBER, DECEMBER, JANUARY

Such things as are green all winter: Holly, ivy, bays, juniper, cypress trees, yew, pineapple trees, fir trees, rosemary, lavender, periwinkle (white, purple and blue varieties), flags, orange trees, lemon trees, and myrtles (if they be stoved), and sweet marjoram, if warm set.

THE LATTER PART OF JANUARY AND FEBRUARY

The mezereon tree (daphne) which then blossoms, crocus (both yellow and grey), primroses, anemones, early tulips, hyacinth, charmaris, fritellaria.

MARCH

Violets (especially the single blue), yellow daffodil, daisy, almond tree in blossom, peach tree in blossom, cornelian tree in blossom, sweetbriar.

APRIL

Violet (the double white), wall-flower, stock gillyflower, cowslip, flower-de-luce (iris), lilies of all kinds, rosemary flowers, tulips, double peony, the pale daffodil, French honeysuckle, cherry tree in blossom, damascene and plum tree in blossom, white thorn in leaf, the lilac tree.

MAY AND JUNE

Pinks of all sorts, especially the blush pink; roses of all kinds, except the musk rose which comes later; honeysuckle, strawberries, bugloss, columbine, the French marigold (flos africanus, also called African marigold). Also, cherry tree in fruit, ribes (currants), figs in fruit, raspberries, vine flowers, lavender in flowers, sweet satyrion (white), herba muscaria, lilium convallium, apple tree in blossom.

JULY

All kinds of gillyflowers, musk roses, the lime tree in blossom, early pears and plums in fruit, gentians, quadlins.

AUGUST

Plums of all sorts, pears, apricots, barberries, filberts, muskmelons, monks-hoods of all colours.

SEPTEMBER

Grapes, apples, poppies of all colours, wardens, quinces.

OCTOBER AND EARLY NOVEMBER

Services, medlars, bullaces, roses that have been cut or removed (pruned) to come late, hollyoaks, and such like.

"And because the breath of flowers is far sweeter in the air (where it comes and goes like the warbling of music) than in the hand, therefore nothing is more fit for that delight, than to know what be the flowers and plants that do best perfume the air."

- ~ *Violets*
- ~ *Musk rose*
- ~ *Sweet briar*
- ~ *Wall-flowers, which are very delightful to be set under a parlor or lower chamber window.*
- ~ *Pinks (carnations) and gillyflowers, especially the matted pink and clove gillyflower.*
- ~ *The flowers of the lime-tree.*
- ~ *Then the honeysuckles, so they be somewhat afar off.*

Getting Started

WHEN originally published in 2010, Flowers for Elizabeth focused on a beautiful, decorative blanket featuring twelve large and twelve small designs, all inspired by the wonderful botanical embroidery of the Elizabethan period. Using wool and cashmere fabric, the motifs are worked onto an ivory background, dramatically sectioned with strapping and bordered with a wide binding in black, reminiscent of the Tudor houses built during the Elizabethan period. This contrast between the monochrome palette of the fabric and the abundance of colour used in the stitching is also borrowed from Tudor times when intricate blackwork smocks, worked onto white or ivory linen, were worn beneath richly coloured outer garments, peeking out at the neck and cuffs to splendid effect.

The Elizabethan passion for floral decoration stemmed largely from their fascination with the relatively new concept of the domestic flower garden. Extant examples of embroidery, coupled with portraiture, ably demonstrate the pleasure they took in decorating themselves and their homes with delights from the garden. The embroidered motifs featured in this book reflect a style popular in pattern books of the time showing gently stylised flowers and fruit emanating from scrolling stems and these can easily be adapted in many ways to suit the individual needs of the embroiderer. Originally worked in surface embroidery, each motif is suited to working in stumpwork, beading, blackwork, cross stitch, whitework and many other stitching styles and techniques.

The blanket is a large project that takes time to complete but each individual motif can be stitched quite quickly. There are numerous other applications for these designs that are only limited by imagination. Stitched on a large scale with Persian, crewel, needlepoint yarn, soft cotton or the heavier weights of perlé cotton, the motifs can be used singly or in groups for blankets, throws and cushions. The small motifs scattered across ivory or coloured fabric would make an elegant throw or a lovely baby blanket.

By reducing the designs to half their original size, they can be worked with several strands of stranded silk or cotton, or the lighter weights of cotton perlé and at this size are ideal for cushions, book covers or framed pictures.

Reducing the size of the designs even further makes them suitable for use with fine threads such as stranded silk or cotton and perfect for the elegant needlework accessories now included in this book. Worked onto silk duchess satin with superb silk threads, each motif is very quick to stitch. The silk embroidery is further enhanced by the addition of sparkling gold paillettes. Five additional small motifs have been used on the reverse of some pinwheels and are included in the pattern section.

WOOL

The majority of wool thread colour numbers listed in the instructions are *Colonial Persian Yarn*. The remaining colour numbers, those threads listed with an **A** before the number, are *Appletons Crewel Wool*. These have been used as substitutes for *Paternayan* colours that have been discontinued in the *Colonial Persian Yarn* range.

The blanket was originally stitched with *Paternayan* wool yarn. Also sold under the name *Paterna*, this three-strand thread is a beautiful, crewel-weight wool with the ideal

level of twist and high resistance to wear. This thread is now produced and sold as *Colonial Persian Yarn*.

The colour range has been reduced slightly and the number 1 has been added before each number eg. *Paternayan* 220 has become *Colonial Persian Yarn* 1220. You may still find skeins of thread available for sale under the *Paternayan* name.

The history of *Paternayan Yarns* dates back to 1916 when two brothers, Harry and Karnick Paternayan, started a Persian carpet repair business. Searching for the best yarn, they found a breed of New Zealand sheep producing soft, white, long-staple wool.

The yarn was slowly spun on special machines in Yorkshire, UK to add strength and resilience, which resisted breakage. A special sheen was also added to their range of different coloured wools, which soon became a favourite for all kinds of needlearts under the name of *Paternayan Bros*.

Today, while the original business has since closed, The *Colonial Needle Company* now owns the trademark, remaining inventory and dye formulas and are continuing to produce many of the classic *Paternayan Bros*. threads using the original colour palette under the name *Colonial Persian Yarn*.

SILK

All the thread numbers listed under the silk heading are **Au Ver à Soie, Soie d'Alger** stranded silk. This is a magnificent French thread sold in skeins of seven strands and is available in more than six hundred lustrous shades. The colours are rich and vibrant and the thread is a delight to use and produces superb results.

THREAD CONVERSION

Appletons CREWEL WOOL	Au Ver à Soie, Soie d'Alger
A101 vy lt purple	1342 lt parma violet
A121 ultra lt terracotta	4643 lt raisin
A244 med olive green	3735 med khaki green
A245 dk olive green	3736 dk khaki green
A256 ultra dk grass green	2145 dk grape green
A472 vy lt autumn yellow	2543 corn
A743 lt bright China blue	1421 vy lt marine blue
A745 med bright China blue	1422 lt marine blue
A754 rose pink	2933 carnation
A942 vy lt bright rose pink	2931 vy lt carnation

Colonial PERSIAN YARN	Au Ver à Soie, Soie d'Alger
1220 black	4106 black
1263 cream	4102 cream
1310 dk grape	5115 med antique iris
1311 med grape	1343 Parma violet
1450 vy dk khaki brown	4536 vy dk beige
1451 dk khaki brown	3836 vy dk mouse
1472 med toast brown	4114 med pigeon grey
1560 dk glacier	4914 med hyacinth
1570 navy blue	1426 dk marine blue
1611 dk hunter green	2135 dk grass green
1612 med hunter green	2134 med grass green
1642 med khaki green	3734 khaki green
1643 khaki green	3733 lt khaki green

Colonial PERSIAN YARN	Au Ver à Soie, Soie d'Alger
1644 lt khaki green	3713 lt grey-green
1651 dk olive green	516 dk leaf green
1652 olive green	2144 med grape green
1690 vy dk loden green	2116 dk pistachio
1691 dk loden green	2126 dk parrot green
1692 med loden green	2115 med pistachio
1693 loden green	2114 pistachio
1694 lt loden green	2132 lt grass green
1695 vy lt loden green	2131 vy lt grass green
1703 butterscotch	542 vy lt golden yellow
1726 vy lt autumn yellow	2514 copper yellow
1730 vy dk honey gold	2246 vy dk colonial gold
1731 dk honey gold	2245 dk colonial gold
1733 honey gold	2515 med copper yellow
1750 vy dk old gold	524 golden olive
1752 med old gold	2234 bronze
1831 dk bittersweet	2636 dk terracotta
1840 vy dk salmon	944 med garnet
1841 dk salmon	926 vy dk peony
1902 med American red	3015 dk geranium
1920 vy dk wood rose	4625 med plum
1925 vy lt wood rose	4621 ultra lt plum
1931 dk rusty rose	2934 med carnation
1933 rusty rose	2932 lt carnation
1940 vy dk cranberry	1026 vy dk rose
1948 ultra vy lt cranberry	4147 ultra lt China rose
1950 vy dk strawberry	1016 vy dk China rose

The Pinwheel

REQUIREMENTS

Fabric

15cm x 30cm wide (6" x 12") piece of ivory silk duchess satin

Supplies

20cm (8") square of thin fusible wadding

10cm (4") embroidery hoop

Gold rayon sewing thread

2mm (1/16") gold paillettes (45)

White glass-head pins (55)

10cm x 20cm wide (4" x 8") piece of thin firm card

Fine black pen

Tracing paper

Heat-soluble fabric marker

Needles

No. 8 crewel

No. 10 crewel

PREPARATION FOR EMBROIDERY

See pages 149–164 for the embroidery designs

We recommend that you read all embroidery and construction information before you begin

All embroidery is worked with ONE strand of thread unless specified

Preparing the fabric

Neaten the edge of the fabric with a machine zigzag or overlock stitch to prevent fraying. Fold the fabric in half and finger press. Work a line of tacking along the crease with contrasting sewing thread.

Transferring the design

> **NOTE:** The embroidery is worked onto the wrong side of the fabric.

Using the black pen trace the front and back designs, circle outlines and placement marks onto the tracing paper. Tape the designs to a lightbox or window. Centre one half of the fabric over the front design and transfer the design only with the heat-soluble marker. Repeat with the back design onto the second half of the fabric. Turn the fabric over and re-position the first half over the front design, ensuring it is centred. Lightly trace the circle outline. Work a line of tacking around the outline with contrasting sewing thread. Repeat with the back design and the second half of the fabric.

Centre the front design in the hoop and tension until the fabric is drum tight. If desired, cut away the fabric with the back design along the tacked centre line.

Once the front design is complete, remove the fabric from the hoop. Mount the back design in the hoop.

EMBROIDERY

Work the embroidery following the instructions for the chosen motifs.

Attach the paillettes with 2–3 straight stitches using the rayon sewing thread.

Use the no. 8 crewel needle for the coral stitch worked during construction and the no. 10 crewel for all other embroidery.

The Scissor Sheath

REQUIREMENTS

Fabric

20cm x 60cm wide (8" x 24") piece of ivory silk duchess satin

Supplies

12.5cm (5") embroidery hoop

Ivory silk sewing thread

Gold rayon sewing thread

2mm (1/16") gold paillettes (25)

15cm x 18cm wide (6" x 7") piece of thin firm card

15cm x 27cm wide (6" x 10 ½") piece of thin fusible wadding

Strong lacing thread

Fine black pen

Tracing paper

Fine heat-soluble fabric marker

Needles

No. 8 crewel
No. 10 crewel

PREPARATION FOR EMBROIDERY

See pages 149–164 for the embroidery designs and page 143 for the cutting layout

We recommend that you read all embroidery and construction information before you begin

All embroidery is worked with ONE strand of thread unless specified

Preparing the fabric

Cut a 20cm (8") square of silk for the sheath front. Neaten the raw edges with a machine zigzag or overlock stitch to prevent fraying.

Transferring the design

NOTE: The embroidery is worked onto the wrong side of the fabric.

Using the black pen transfer the chosen design, outline shaping and placement marks onto the tracing paper. Centre the design under the square of silk, aligning the placement marks with the straight grain and, using a lightbox or window, transfer the design only onto the wrong side of the fabric using the heat-soluble marker. Turn the fabric over and re-position over the design. On the right side of the fabric, lightly mark the outline shaping. Work a line of tacking around the outline shaping on the fabric using contrasting sewing thread. Place the fabric in the 12.5cm (5") hoop and tension until drum tight, taking care not to distort the tacked outline.

EMBROIDERY

Work the embroidery following the instructions for the chosen motif.

Attach the paillettes with 2–3 straight stitches using the rayon sewing thread.

Use the no. 8 crewel needle for the corded coral stitch worked during construction and the no. 10 crewel for all other embroidery.

The Needlebook

REQUIREMENTS

Fabric

25cm x 60cm wide (10" x 24") piece of ivory silk duchess satin

10cm x 40cm wide (4" x 16") piece of cream wool flannel

Supplies

15cm (6") embroidery hoop

Clear glass pebble bead (1)

Ivory silk sewing thread

Gold rayon sewing thread

2mm (¹⁄₁₆") gold paillettes (40)

29.5cm x 21cm wide (A4) piece of thin firm card

15cm x 40cm wide (6" x 16") piece of thin fusible wadding

Strong lacing thread

Pinking shears

Craft glue

Fine black pen

Tracing paper

Fine heat-soluble fabric marker

Needles

No. 8 crewel
No. 10 crewel

PREPARATION FOR EMBROIDERY

See pages 149–164 for the embroidery designs and page 144 for the cutting layout

We recommend that you read all embroidery and construction information before you begin

All embroidery is worked with ONE strand of thread unless specified

Preparing the fabric

Cut one 20cm (8") square of silk for the front. Neaten the raw edges with a machine zigzag or overlock stitch to prevent fraying.

Transferring the design

> **NOTE:** The embroidery is worked onto the wrong side of the fabric.

Using the black pen transfer the chosen design, outline shaping and placement marks onto the tracing paper.

Centre the design under the square of silk, aligning the placement marks with the straight grain and, using a lightbox or window, transfer the design only onto the wrong side of the fabric using the heat-soluble marker. Turn the fabric over and re-position over the design. On the right side of the fabric, lightly mark the outline shaping. Work a line of tacking around the outline shaping on the fabric using contrasting sewing thread. Place the fabric in the 15cm (6") embroidery hoop and tension until drum tight, taking care not to distort the tacked outlines.

EMBROIDERY

Work the embroidery following the instructions for the chosen motif.

Attach the paillettes with 2–3 straight stitches using the rayon sewing thread.

Use the no. 8 crewel needle for the corded coral stitch worked during construction and the no. 10 crewel for all other embroidery.

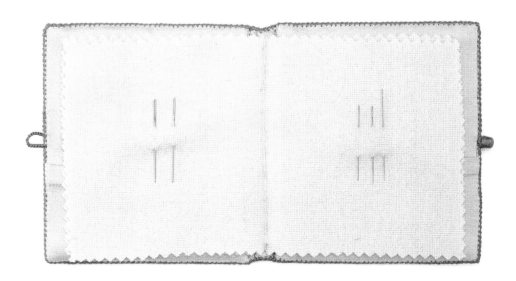

The Blanket

REQUIREMENTS

Fabric

127cm x 112cm wide (50" x 44") ivory wool and cashmere velour

1m x 140cm wide (1yd 13" x 55") black wool and cashmere velour

127cm x 112cm wide (50" x 44") cream twill

Supplies

22cm x 1.5cm deep (8½" x ⅝") wooden hoop

Black sewing thread

Tracing paper

Fine black pen

White dressmaker's pencil

Heat-soluble fabric marker

Threads and Needles

To complete the blanket you will need the threads listed on page 25 and one skein of each wool thread listed on page 15.

CUTTING OUT

This blanket is made from wool and cashmere velour. The fabric is woven then brushed to raise a smooth velour surface on one side, a process that meshes the fibres and prevents the raw edges of the fabric unravelling. This makes it impossible to pull a thread to obtain a straight edge and very difficult to cut straight.

The best way to divide the fabric into the required strips is by tearing. Make a straight 2.5cm (1") cut into the selvedge at the required measurement. Hold each edge and quickly tear across the width, stopping 1cm (⅜") from the remaining selvedge. Cut to the edge.

If you are using an alternate fabric that does not share this characteristic, you may need to cut the strips wider and make a small hem down each side of each strip.

Divide the black wool and cashmere fabric into the following strips:

Two each, 15cm x 140cm wide (6" x 55")

Two each, 15cm x 125cm wide (6" x 49¼")

Two each, 4cm x 84cm wide (1½" x 33")

Two each, 4cm x 99cm wide (1½" x 39")

Two each, 2.5cm x 117cm wide (1" x 46")

Four each, 2.5cm x 82cm wide (1" x 32")

Four each, 2.5cm x 39cm wide (1" x 15⅜")

Put aside the 15cm (6") wide strips. These are used to bind the blanket once it is complete.

PREPARATION FOR EMBROIDERY

Border

With dark fabrics of this type, it is easy to inadvertently cut the fabric with the wrong side facing. Before cutting the angles for the mitres, use a white dressmaker's pencil and mark the wrong side of each strip.

Use the following strips:

Two, 4cm x 84cm wide (1½" x 33")

Two, 4cm x 99cm wide (1½" x 39")

At each end of each strip, fold the fabric so that the short edge is aligned with the long edge (diag 1).

Press the fold then open out. Cut along the foldline. Each end of each strip should be cut at an opposite angle (diag 2).

With the right sides of the strips together, pin and stitch the mitred corners to form a rectangle using a 1cm (⅜") seam allowance and the black sewing thread. Press the seams open and trim the seam allowance on the outer edges (diag 3).

Measure in 15cm (6") from each raw edge of the ivory velour and mark with the fabric marker. With the fabric on a flat surface, position the border, with right side uppermost, onto the right side of the ivory velour, aligning the outer edge with the marks. Pin and tack in place around the outer edge. Remove any visible marks with a hair dryer.

Lattice

Use the following strips:

Two, 2.5cm x 117cm wide (1" x 46")

Four, 2.5cm x 82cm wide (1" x 32")

Four, 2.5cm x 39cm wide (1" x 15⅜")

Beginning at the upper left-hand corner, tuck the end of one long strip under the inner edge of the border, centering the strip to the corner seam. Pin in place through all fabric layers (diag 4).

Lay the strip diagonally across the fabric and pin in place along the length. Trim away any excess from the end, ensuring that there is enough fabric to secure the strip under the lower right-hand corner of the border. Tuck the remaining end under the inner edge of the border, again centering the strip to the mitre seam and pin in place through all layers. Tack in place close to both edges. Repeat for the remaining long diagonal strip, crossing the first at the centre. Mark the centre point of the diamond formed by the two crossed strips. From this point, measure out 19.3cm (7 ⅝") in each direction and mark this point at the centre of each strip. From this marked point, measure out 19.3cm (7 ⅝") again and mark at the centre of each strip. You should now have five points marked along each of the long strips, both sharing the centre mark. Aligning the centre of the remaining strips with the marks and ensuring that each new strip is parallel to the previous, pin and tack in place, tucking the ends under the inner edge of the border and trimming away any excess fabric. Adjust as necessary.

Tack the black border in place around the inner edge.

BORDER AND LATTICE EMBROIDERY

Threads and needles

Colonial Persian yarn

A = 220 black (3)

B = 1750 vy dk old gold (10)

Needles

No. 18 chenille

No. 22 chenille

Border

The border is completed before working the remainder of the embroidery.

Using two strands of **B** and the no. 18 chenille needle, work zigzag chain around the outer and inner edges of the border. Using one strand of **B** and the no. 22 chenille needle, work fly stitch-detached chain combination around the outer edges of the border.

Lattice

The lattice embroidery is worked after all other embroidery is complete.

Using one strand of **B** and the no. 22 chenille needle, work twisted chain stitch along both edges of each strip, forming a diamond at the point that the strips cross.

Work a detached chain cross at the centre of each intersection, using one strand of the same thread. Stitch a French knot at the centre of the cross, between each arm of the cross and 5mm (³⁄₁₆") from each point of the diamond using one strand of **B**. Using one strand of **A**, work running stitch along each edge of each strip, approximately 3mm (⅛") from the twisted chain stitch edge. Remove the tacking.

TRANSFERRING THE DESIGNS

See pages 149–164 for the embroidery designs.

The designs are best transferred one at a time. Each one is embroidered before the next design is transferred.

Refer to the close-up photograph for placement.

Using the black pen, trace the design onto the tracing paper. Tape the tracing to a light box. With the right side facing, centre a diamond over the tracing and pin in place. Using the heat-soluble marker, trace the design onto the fabric. All flower embroidery is worked in the hoop.

ZIGZAG CHAIN STITCH

A variation of chain stitch, zigzag chain is a wider stitch, ideal for appliquéing fabrics. It makes an attractive zigzag line.

Bring the needle to the front at A just outside the corner of the border.

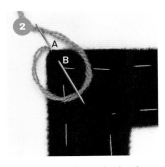

Take the needle to the back at A, emerge at B, 5mm (³⁄₁₆") into the border, ensuring the thread is under the needle.

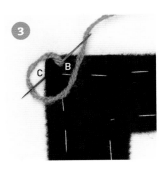

Pull the thread through. Take the needle to the back at B. Emerge at C, just outside the border, ensuring the thread is under the needle.

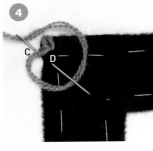

Pull the thread through. Take the needle to the back at C. Emerge at D, ensuring that the thread is under the needle.

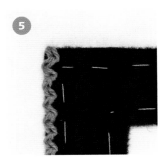

Continue working in this manner.

FLY STITCH - DETACHED CHAIN COMBINATION

This variation of fly stitch is anchored with a detached chain rather than a straight stitch.

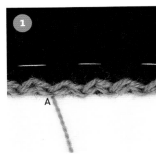

Bring the thread to the front at A, an outer point of the zigzag chain.

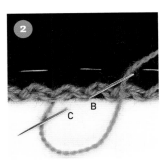

Take the needle to the back at B, the next point, and emerge at C, approximately 5mm (³⁄₁₆") from the edge. Ensure the thread is under the needle.

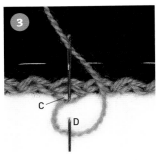

Pull the thread through. Take the needle to the back at C and emerge at D, 5mm (³⁄₁₆") from C. Ensure that the thread is under the needle.

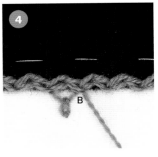

Pull the thread through. Take the needle to the back over the loop and emerge at B.

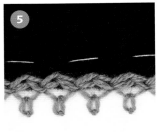

Continue working along the zigzag chain in this manner.

TWISTED CHAIN STITCH

Twisted chain is another stitch ideal for appliquéing fabrics. It creates a textured, rope-like line of stitching.

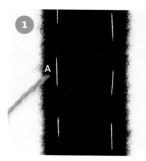

Bring the thread to the front at A, close to the edge of the lattice strip.

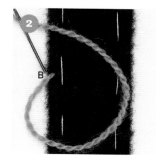

Take the needle to the back at B, just outside the lattice strip. Form a loop with the emerging thread.

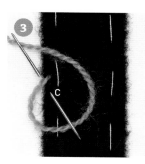

Bring the needle to the front at C, close to the edge of the lattice strip. Ensure the thread is under the needle.

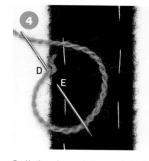

Pull the thread through. Take the needle to the back at D, just outside the lattice strip. Emerge at E, ensuring the thread is under the needle.

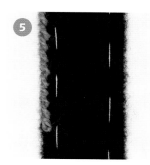

Pull the thread through. Continue working in this manner to the end of the line. Take the thread to the back over the last loop.

An Elizabethan
Garden

Borage & Honeysuckle

—— DIRECTNESS + DEVOTION ——

Borage

BORAGO OFFICINALIS

ONE of the most popular floral motifs in Elizabethan embroidery, borage has spectacular, star shaped flowers with a prominent coned centre. The petals are an intense blue that contrasts with the stark black anthers and white of the flower centre. Leaves are large, dark green and both leaves and stem are covered in fine bristles.

Borage is an annual herb indigenous to the Middle East, particularly Syria. Its medicinal and culinary value has been recognised for at least 2000 years. Like many plants, it was introduced to England by the Romans and was valued as a treatment for melancholy as it was said to 'lighten the spirits'. Historically associated with courage, it is mentioned in 13th century English writings.

Also known as 'star flower', borage was used in various ways by the Elizabethans. As well as its value as a tonic, the leaves were used in salads, having a taste similar to cucumber. The flower has a sweet honey taste and, being one of the few truly blue-coloured edible things, was popular as a garnish on desserts.

The plant grows to a height of 60–100cm (2–3 ft) and easily self-seeds, sending up seedlings between bricks in pathways and other unlikely places. If unchecked it can spread prolifically, but is easy to remove when growing where unwanted. In a mild climate it will provide flowers continuously throughout the year. It makes a worthwhile addition to any garden.

The entry in Gerard's Herball or General Historie of Plantes 1633 reads:

*"Borago. Borage.
...Those of our time do vse the floures in sallads, to exhilerate and make the mind glad... The leaues boyled among other pot-herbes do much preuaile in making the belly soluble..."*

Honeysuckle

LONICERA PERICLYMENUM

ANOTHER of the most commonly used flower motifs in Elizabethan embroidery, honeysuckle, or woodbine, combines a unique flower form with a delightful fragrance.

Native to England, honeysuckle can be found growing in hedges and woodlands throughout the country. It has beautiful clusters of tubular flowers, soft yellow that are often flushed with red or purple. Each bud opens to a paler flower with long arching stamens that curl elegantly from the flower throat. Flowering from early summer, the heady fragrance fills the air on warm evenings or after a rain shower. A hardy, climbing plant, the stems are reddish-green when young but age to a woody brown. Bright green leaves contrast beautifully with both the flowers and the stems. Once the flowers are spent, bright berries form in clusters.

Honeysuckle will tolerate poor soils and should be grown in a sunny spot where it can climb happily against a wall, fence, pergola or tree trunk.

The Elizabethan herbalist Nicholas Culpepper wrote in his Complete Herbal 1653:

"It is fitting a conserve made of the (honeysuckle) flowers should be kept in every gentlewoman's house; I know no better cure for the asthma than this besides it takes away the evil of the spleen: provokes urine, procures speedy delivery of women in travail, relieves cramps, convulsions, and palsies, and whatsoever griefs come of cold or obstructed perspiration; if you make use of it as an ointment, it will clear the skin of morphew, freckles, and sunburnings, or whatever else discolors it, and then the maids will love it."

Borage &
Honeysuckle

THIS DESIGN USES

French knot • Long and short stitch • Outline stitch • Satin stitch
Satin stitch padding • Split stitch • Stem stitch • Straight stitch • Whipping

THREADS

Wool

A = 1220 black
B = 1263 cream
C = 1311 med grape
D = 1560 dk glacier
E = 1644 lt khaki green
F = A256 ultra dk grass green
G = 1652 olive green
H = 1691 dk loden green
I = 1695 vy lt loden green
J = A472 vy lt autumn yellow
K = 1730 vy dk old gold
L = 1733 honey gold
M = 1750 vy dk old gold
N = 1752 med old gold
O = 1831 dk bittersweet
P = 1902 med American red

Silk

A = 4106 black
B = 4102 cream
C = 1343 Parma violet
D = 4914 med hyacinth
E = 3713 lt grey-green
F = 2145 dk grape green
G = 2144 med grape green
H = 2126 dk parrot green
I = 2131 vy lt grass green
J = 2543 corn
K = 2246 vy dk colonial gold
L = 2515 med copper yellow
M = 524 golden olive
N = 2234 bronze
O = 2636 dk terracotta
P = 3015 dk geranium

ORDER OF WORK

All embroidery is worked with one strand of thread.

Main stems

Using **K**, work the main stem in outline stitch beginning at the top of the design, below the borage buds. Stitch down around the curving tip and back to the starting point.

Work the borage stems in outline stitch using **H**. Using **E**, whip the upper part of the main stem and the borage stems following the close-up photograph.

Honeysuckle

Stems

Stitch the honeysuckle stems in outline stitch using **K**.

Leaves

Beginning at the outer edge, fill each leaf with rows of split stitch using **G**. Stitch the centre vein on each leaf in split stitch using **F**.

Flowers

Using the photograph as a guide to colour placement, work the closed flowers in **J**, **L** or **N**. Outline each with split stitch, then fill with satin stitch padding along the length. Cover the padding with satin stitch, working across the shape.

Stitch the lower part of each open flower in the same manner using **L**. Outline the open petals in split stitch using **J**. Work the petals in long and short stitch using **J**. Stitch several straight stitch highlights from the centre of the flower using **L**. Changing to **I**, stitch the stamens in stem stitch. Work each stamen tip with two small straight stitches worked into the same holes using **O**. Using **F**, work several straight stitches at the base of each flower as indicated in the photograph.

Borage

Leaf

Outline the leaf in split stitch using **G**. Fill the leaf with long and short stitch using **F** and **G**. Work the leaf veins in outline stitch using **K**.

Flowers and buds

Outline each flower petal in split stitch using **C** or **D**. Fill the petals with satin stitch using **D** for the full face flower and open bud and **C** and **D** for the side view flower. Work a small straight stitch using **C** at the tips of the open bud petals. Work a star of straight stitches using **B** at the centre of the full face flower. Stitch a second, smaller star in straight stitch using **A** (diag 1).

Work a French knot in the centre using **A**.

Embroider the centre of the side view flower in satin stitch using **A** and **B** (diag 2).

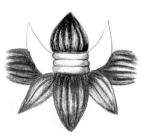

Stitch the sepals in satin stitch using **H**.

Outline each closed bud with split stitch using **H**. Fill with satin stitch padding and cover with satin stitch using the same colour. Work one or two straight stitches over each bud as shown using **E**. Stitch a small straight stitch at the tip of each bud using **P**.

Curlicues

Using **M**, stitch each curl using one row of stem and one row of outline stitch for the wool and one row of outline or stem stitch for the silk.

OUTLINE STITCH

Ideal for creating straight or curved lines, outline stitch is smooth and untextured when worked with s-twist threads.

1. Bring the thread to the front at A at the left-hand end of the line.

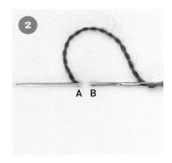

2. Take the needle to the back at B and re-emerge at A. Ensure that the thread is above the needle.

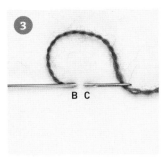

3. Pull the thread through. Take the needle to the back at C and re-emerge at B, keeping the thread above the needle.

4. Pull the thread through. Continue working in this manner to the end of the line.

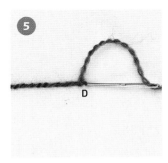

5. Take the thread to the back at D and secure.

STEM STITCH

Another great line stitch, stem is more textured when worked with s-twist threads.

1. Bring the thread to the front at A at the left-hand end of the line.

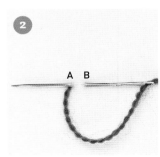

2. Take the needle to the back at B and re-emerge at A. Ensure that the thread is below the needle.

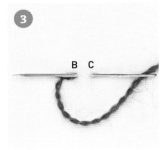

3. Pull the thread through. Take the needle to the back at C and re-emerge at B, again keeping the thread below the needle.

4. Pull the thread through. Continue working in this manner to the end of the line.

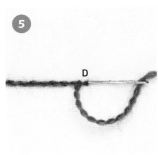

5. Take the thread to the back at D and secure.

HONEYSUCKLE MOTIF

THIS DESIGN USES

Outline stitch • Satin stitch padding • Split stitch

THREADS

Wool

A = 1652 olive green
B = A256 ultra dk grass green
C = 1752 med old gold
D = A472 vy lt autumn yellow
E = 1730 vy dk honey gold

Silk

A = 2144 med grape green
B = 2145 dk grape green
C = 2234 bronze
D = 2543 corn
E = 2246 vy dk colonial gold

ORDER OF WORK

All embroidery is worked with one strand of thread.

Stem

Stitch the stem in outline stitch using **E**.

Leaves

Beginning at the outer edge, fill each leaf with rows of split stitch using **A**. Stitch the centre vein on each leaf with split stitch using **B**.

Flowers

Using **C**, outline the inner buds with split stitch and fill with satin stitch padding along the length. Cover the padding with satin stitch, working across the shape. Stitch the outer buds in the same manner using **D**. Using **A**, work the receptacle at the base of the buds with satin stitch.

Poppy & Columbine

PLEASURE + FOLLY

Poppy

PAPAVER RHOEAS

THE bright red corn or field poppy is native to much of Europe. As the name implies it grows wild in the fields, often amongst wheat or corn crops where it forms a startling display. It is an annual flower that has single, rich, scarlet flowers with a dark eye at the base of each petal. The flower has no nectar but bees flock to collect the pollen and the papery seed capsules are often used as a winter home by beetles.

A poppy plant can produce up to 17,000 seeds in one year and each seed can lie dormant for up to 40 years. Once the soil is disturbed, the seed starts to grow and it is not unusual for a large patch of poppies to appear where, in previous years, there have been none.

The opium or lettuce poppy, *Papaver somnifera*, was also found in Elizabethan gardens. Introduced by the Romans, this plant flowered in several colours, including striped varieties. The poppy was the sacred plant of Ceres, the Roman Goddess of Crops, and her statue was often adorned by garlands made from poppies and barley.

Although not as popular in Elizabethan embroidery as many other flowers, the poppy added a splash of strong red that worked particularly well with the intense blues of borage and cornflowers.

The entry in Gerard's Herball or General Historie of Plantes 1633 reads:

"Papauer. Garden Poppies.
...This seed, as Galen saith in his booke of the Faculties of nourishments, is good to season bread with; but the white is better than the black. He also addeth, that the same is cold and causeth sleepe, and yeeldeth no commendable nourishment to the body; it is often vsed in comfits, serued at the table with other iunketting dishes. The oile which is pressed out of it is pleasant and delightfull to be eaten, and is taken with bread or any other waies in meat, without any sence of cooling."

Columbine

AQUILEGIA VULGARIS

ANOTHER plant with an intriguing flower form, the columbine or granny's bonnet is a native of England and was originally found in wet woodlands, fens and grasslands. This very attractive perennial plant soon made its way into the home garden and onto the fabric of the embroiderer. Columbines were very popular motifs for the Elizabethan embroiderer and appear in both blackwork and polychrome embroidery.

The columbine is a tall, upright plant with a clump of greyish green divided leaves at the base. It will tolerate full sun or some shade and prefers moist, free draining soil. Although wild columbines were blue, they quickly became available in shades from white through pink to dark purple. The spurred flowers are held on long, bare stems and the distinctive blooms are bell shaped with each petal modified into an elongated nectar spur. This gives each petal the appearance of a tiny bird and for this reason, the flower is associated with the Dove of the Holy Spirit.

Flowering begins in spring and continues for several months. A single plant produces large amounts of seed and will happily self-sow in a mild climate. The seed was said to hasten labour!

The Shepherd's Calender – Edmund Spenser 1579

Bring hether the Pinke and purple Cullambine
With Gelliflowres:
Bring Coronations and Sops in Wine,
Worn of Paramours.
Strowe me the ground with Daffadowndillies,
And Cowslips, and Kingcups and loved Lillies:
The pretie Paunce
And the Chevisaunce
Shall match the fayre flower Delice.

Poppy &
Columbine

Wool

A = 1310 dk grape
B = 1450 vy dk khaki brown
C = 1472 med toast brown
D = A244 med olive green
E = 1643 khaki green
F = 1652 olive green
G = 1691 dk loden green
H = 1726 vy lt autumn yellow
I = 1750 vy dk old gold
J = 1840 vy dk salmon
K = 1841 dk salmon
L = 1931 dk rusty rose

Silk

A = 5115 med antique iris
B = 4536 vy dk beige
C = 4114 med pigeon grey
D = 3735 med khaki green
E = 3733 lt khaki green
F = 2144 med grape green
G = 2126 dk parrot green
H = 2514 copper yellow
I = 524 golden olive
J = 944 med garnet
K = 926 vy dk peony
L = 2934 med carnation

THIS DESIGN USES

Blanket stitch • French knot • Long and short blanket stitch
Long and short stitch • Outline stitch • Satin stitch • Satin stitch padding
Split stitch • Stem stitch • Straight stitch

long and short stitch, leaving a space, as shown in the photograph, for the darker petal markings. Work the dark markings in long and short stitch using **B**. Using **E**, fill the two sections of the poppy centre with satin stitch (diag 2).

Work straight stitches over the oval section of the centre using **L**, ensuring that each stitch crosses at the centre (diag 3).

Cut a 25cm (10") length of **B**. Gently separate the two plies that make up the strand. Thread one into the needle and work another layer of straight stitches, again ensuring that they cross at the centre.

Columbine

Leaves

Outline all the leaves in split stitch using **G**. Fill the small leaf using rows of split stitch in the same colour. Fill the large leaves with satin stitch using **G**. Embroider the leaf veins in stem stitch using **F**.

Flowers and bud

Embroider the flower and bud stems in stem and outline stitch using **G**. Work a split stitch outline around the large lower flower petals and lower section of the bud using **A**. Fill each outlined area with satin stitch padding across the shapes, then cover with satin stitch using **A**. Stitch along the upper, tubular part of each petal in split stitch using **A**. Cover the split stitch with satin stitch (diag 4).

Embroider the small lighter petals and petal highlights in straight stitch using **C**.

Work the flower stamens in straight stitch and French knots using **H**.

Curlicues

Using **I**, stitch each curl using one row of stem and one row of outline stitch for the wool and one row of outline or stem stitch for the silk.

ORDER OF WORK

All embroidery is worked with one strand of thread.

Main stem

Using **B**, work the main stem in outline stitch, beginning below the open poppy. Stitch down around the curving tip and back to the starting point.

Poppy

Stem

Work a single line of outline stitch using **B** to the partially opened flower.

Leaves

Outline each leaf in split stitch using **E**. Fill each leaf with long and short stitch using **D** and **E**. Stitch each leaf vein in stem stitch using **D**.

Bud

Embroider the bud stem in outline stitch using **E**. Using the same thread, work split stitch around the bud outline. Fill the lower half of the bud with rows of split stitch using **E**. With the same colour, fill the upper half with satin stitch padding along the length. Cover with satin stitch, working from the outer edge towards the centre. Using **D**, work small straight stitches over the bud as shown (diag 1).

Flowers

Stitch around the outer edge of each petal with long and short blanket stitch or blanket stitch using **K**, varying the length of the stitches to fill the required space. Using **J**, fill the base of each petal with

diag 1

diag 2

diag 3

diag 4

LONG AND SHORT BLANKET STITCH PETALS

Long and short blanket stitch is an excellent filling stitch and creates a pretty beaded edge.

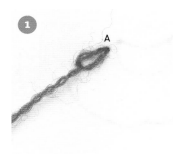

1 Bring the thread to the front at A. Work a detached chain without anchoring the stitch.

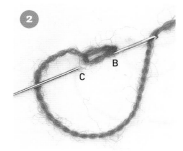

2 Take the needle to the back at B and emerge at C, ensuring that the thread is under the needle.

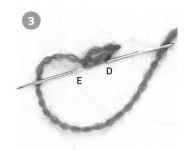

3 Pull the thread through. Take the needle to the back at D and emerge at E, again ensuring that the thread is under the needle.

4 Pull the thread through. Continue working across the petal, alternating the length of each stitch.

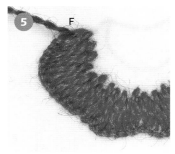

5 Changing colour, bring the thread to the front at F, splitting the stitch of the previous row.

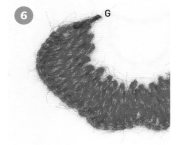

6 Take the needle to the back at G, close to the base of the petal.

7 Continue working long and short stitches across the petal.

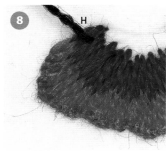

8 Changing colour, bring the thread to the front at H, splitting the stitch of the previous row.

9 Work across the petal, alternating the length of each stitch and filling the remaining space.

POPPY MOTIF

THIS DESIGN USES

Blanket stitch • Long and short blanket stitch
Long and short stitch • Outline stitch • Split stitch

THREADS

Wool

A = *1750 vy dk old gold*
B = *1841 dk salmon*
C = *1840 vy dk salmon*
D = *1643 khaki green*
E = *A244 med olive green*
F = *1450 vy dk khaki brown*

Silk

A = *524 golden olive*
B = *926 vy dk peony*
C = *944 med garnet*
D = *3733 lt khaki green*
E = *3735 med khaki green*
F = *4536 vy dk beige*

ORDER OF WORK

All embroidery is worked with one strand of thread.

Stem

Stitch the stem in outline stitch using **F**.

Leaf

Outline the leaf with split stitch using **D**. Fill each side with long and short stitch, beginning on the outer edge with **D** and shading into **E** near the vein.

Flower

Fill the two back petals with close blanket stitch or long and short blanket stitch using **B**. Fill the outer area of the centre and front petals in the same manner then fill the remaining area with long and short stitch shading from **C** to **F**.

Curlicue

Stitch the curlicue with outline stitch using **A**.

Raspberry & Tulip

—— REMORSE + FAME ——

Raspberry

RUBUS IDAEUS

RASPBERRIES are a member of the rose family and there are more than 200 species of red raspberries found in Europe. The name 'raspberry' is something of a misnomer as the fruit is not a berry at all but a collection of druplets, each one containing a seed.

Red raspberries are thought to have originated in Turkey and they are mentioned in Roman records going back to the 4th century AD. The Romans spread the cultivation of the fruit through Europe, but it was the English who cultivated, hybridised and improved the varieties throughout the Middle Ages.

Raspberries can be grown in most temperate areas but they will not tolerate very hot summers. The fruit is produced in the summer on long canes that are trained onto a trellis, fence or wire and are cut back to ground level after picking. New canes will grow and can be trained into the desired shape.

In Elizabethan times, raspberries were "layde to the inflammation in the eyes" to "quencheth such hoate burninges" and they were also used in desserts.

Many cultures consider the raspberry to be a 'fruit of love' but it is more commonly used during pregnancy for combating morning sickness.

Raspberry Wine

Take four Gallons of Deal wine, put it into an earthen jugg; put to it four Gallons of Rasberries; let them stand so infusing seven days; then press it out gently; Then infuse as many more Rasberries seven days longer, and so three times if you please; put to it as much fine Sugar as will make it pleasant; Put it into a Runlet close stopped, let it stand still till it is fine; and then draw it into bottles, and keep it till it be fine.

Tulip

TULIPA SPECIES

TULIPS first appeared in England in 1578 but they did not initially evoke the type of hysteria that was to come in later years in the Netherlands.

Shakespeare, a contemporary of Elizabeth I and fond of using popular flowers in his writings, did not mention them in any of his plays.

Tulips are most often associated with the Netherlands, however they originated in Turkey and parts of western and central Europe. They grow best in rich fertile soil in open, sunny locations and they should be protected from strong winds and too much moisture. Tulip varieties of the 16th and 17th centuries had pointed petals that often curved out or were 'reflexed'. The most valued bulbs were those that produced flowers with multiple colours, stripes, specks or flaming, caused by the mosaic virus. Early tulips also had shorter stems than modern varieties.

For the Elizabethan embroiderer, the tulip offered wonderful colours and an elegance and clarity of form that was not found in many other flowers. The popular technique of stitching flower slips that were cut out and attached to other fabrics was perfectly suited to the simple shape of the tulip.

Paradisus in Sole Paradisus Terrestris

Above and beyond all others, the Tulipas may be so matched, one colour answering and setting of another, that the place where they stand may resemble a peece of curious needlework...

JOHN PARKINSON, 1629

Raspberry & Tulip

THIS DESIGN USES

Detached chain • French knot • Ghiordes knot • Long and short stitch
Outline stitch • Satin stitch • Satin stitch padding • Split stitch
Stem stitch • Straight stitch

THREADS

Wool

A = 1263 cream
B = 1310 dk grape
C = 1311 med grape
D = A101 vy lt purple
E = 1472 med toast brown
F = A244 med olive green
G = 1642 med khaki green
H = 1643 khaki green
I = 1651 dk olive green
J = 1652 olive green
K = 1691 dk loden green
L = 1692 med loden green
M = 1695 vy lt loden green
N = 1726 vy lt autumn yellow
O = 1750 vy dk old gold
P = A942 vy lt bright rose pink
Q = 1948 ultra vy lt cranberry
R = 1950 vy dk strawberry

Silk

A = 4102 cream
B = 5115 med antique iris
C = 1343 Parma violet
D = 1342 lt Parma violet
E = 4114 med pigeon grey
F = 3735 med khaki green
G = 3734 khaki green
H = 3733 lt khaki green
I = 516 dk leaf green
J = 2144 med grape green
K = 2126 dk parrot green
L = 2115 med pistachio
M = 2131 vy lt grass green
N = 2514 copper yellow
O = 524 golden olive
P = 2931 vy lt carnation
Q = 4147 ultra lt China rose
R = 1016 vy dk China rose

ORDER OF WORK

All embroidery is worked with one strand of thread unless specified.

Main stem

Using **I**, work the main stem in stem stitch, beginning below the large tulip. Stitch down around the curving tip and back to the starting point.

Tulip

Stems

Using **F**, work two rows of stem stitch along each section of the stem for the small tulip. Cover with satin stitch using the same thread. Embroider the stem for the large tulip in the same manner using **J** (diag 1).

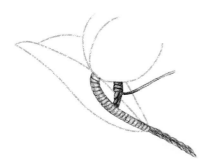

Leaves

Outline the lower leaf in split stitch using **J**. Using the photograph as a guide for colour placement, fill the leaf with rows of split stitch using **J** and **H**. Outline the upper leaf in split stitch using **J**. Fill the leaf with rows of split stitch using **J** and **G**. Stitch the centre veins in split stitch using **F**.

Flowers

Outline the three large tulip petals in split stitch using **D** and the smaller back petal using **C**. Fill the small petal with satin stitch using **C**. Fill the three large petals in long and short stitch using **D** and **C**. Stitch highlights in straight stitch using **A** referring to the close-up photograph.

Outline the small tulip in split stitch using **C**. Fill the petals with long and short stitch in the same colour. Using **B**, work the dark areas at the base of the petals and the line between the petals in straight stitch. Using **D**, embroider the petal highlights in straight stitch.

Raspberry

Stems

Embroider the leaf stems and the stem curl above the berries in stem stitch using **I**.

Leaves

Using **L**, outline each leaf with split stitch. Using the same colour, fill each half of each leaf with satin stitch, worked at an angle.

Flowers and bud

Outline each petal with split stitch using **A**. Fill the petals of the large flower with satin stitch padding. Work satin stitch over the petals using **A**. Using **Q**, work several straight stitches at the base of each petal. Using **P**, work a single straight stitch at the base of each petal of the large flower and the three back petals of the smaller flower. Fill the centres of the two open flowers with Ghiordes knots using two strands of **N**. Work a French knot at the centre of the large flower using **J**. Work three small straight stitches between each flower petal of the large flower using **L**. Stitch the calyx of the flower bud with straight stitch using **L**.

Berries

Beginning at the top of the stem, fill the first berry with French knots using one strand each of **H** and **M** together in the needle. Work the knots at the top of the second berry with a combination of **M** and **R**. Stitch the remaining knots with two strands of **R**.

Fill the remaining berries with French knots using two strands of **R**. Scatter French knots stitched with one strand of **R** and one of **E** over the lower half of the fifth berry (diag 2).

Stitch the berry sepals with detached chain using two strands of **K**.

Curlicues

Using **O**, embroider each curl with one row of stem and one row of outline stitch for the wool and one row of outline or stem stitch for the silk.

GHIORDES KNOT

Used for centuries in rug making, Ghiordes knot creates a raised tufted surface.

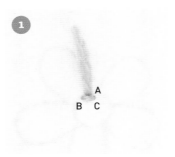

1 Take the needle to the back at A, leaving a tail. Bring the thread to the front at B. Make a small stitch from B to C.

2 Bring the needle to the front at D, beside A.

3 Take the needle to the back at E, leaving a loop on the surface.

4 Bring the thread to the front at C and make a small stitch from C to F.

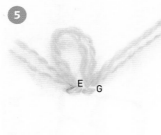

5 Bring the thread to the front at G, beside E.

6 Continue working close rows in this manner until the space is filled. Using sharp scissors, cut the loops and trim to the required height.

7 Using a brush or the tip of the needle, tease out the thread fibres.

RASPBERRY MOTIF

THIS DESIGN USES

Detached chain • French knot • Satin stitch
Split stitch • Stem stitch

THREADS

Wool

A = 1950 vy dk strawberry
B = 1692 med loden green
C = 1691 dk loden green
D = 1695 vy lt loden green
E = 1643 khaki green
F = A244 med olive green
G = 1472 med toast brown

Silk

A = 1016 vy dk China rose
B = 2115 med pistachio
C = 2126 dk parrot green
D = 2131 vy lt grass green
E = 3733 lt khaki green
F = 3735 med khaki green
G = 4144 med pigeon grey

ORDER OF WORK

All embroidery is worked with one strand of thread unless specified.

Stem

Stitch the stem, including the curlicue at the tip and the leaf stem, with stem stitch using **F**.

Leaf

Outline the leaf with split stitch and cover each half with angled satin stitch using **B**.

Berries

Beginning at the top of the stem, fill the first berry with French knots using one strand of **E** and **D** together in the needle. Work the knots at the top of the second berry with a combination of **D** and **A** and the remaining berry with two strands of **A**. Fill the lower berries with French knots using two strands of **A** and scatter knots worked with **G** and **A** together in the needle over the right-hand berry.

Stitch the berry sepals with detached chain using two strands of **C**.

Primrose
& Thistle

———— YOUTH + NOBILITY ————

Primrose

PRIMULA VULGARIS

THE common or English primrose is native to western and southern Europe and was originally found in open woods and shaded hedgerows.

The name comes from old French *primerose* or medieval Latin *prima rosa*, meaning 'first rose' as it is one of the first flowers to open in the spring. An herbaceous perennial, it is low growing with a rosette of glossy leaves with the flowers born singly on long stems.

The flowers of the common primrose are pale green-yellow with a darker yellow eye at the centre. Other varieties of primrose come in shades of yellow, white, pink, red and purple.

One of the favourite flowers of Elizabethan gardeners and embroiderers, the Hose-in-Hose mutation was particularly valued. In this variant form of the common primrose, the calyx of the flower is transformed into a second petaloid structure, giving the impression of a flower within a flower. The name comes from the way some Elizabethan gentlemen wore their stockings; one inside the other with the outer stocking turned down. The first recorded mention of this variant is in John Gerard's 1597 herbal.

The cowslip (*Primula veris*) was another variety of primrose valued in the 16th century. It was used to make wine, jam, tea and ointment and was thought to cure a number of ailments. Also known as Palsywort, it was used to treat spasms, cramps, rheumatic pain and paralysis. The root was used to treat coughs and bronchitis, while the leaves were used to heal wounds and the flowers were eaten to strengthen the brain. Leaves were also eaten in salads and mixed with other herbs to use as a stuffing for meat.

Thistle

ONOPORDUM ACANTHIUM

THISTLE is the common name for a group of plants that carry leaves with sharp prickles on the margins. They often have prickles all over the plant that can inflict a stinging wound when touched. The prickles are designed to protect the plant from animals who would otherwise feed on it.

In the language of flowers, the thistle is an ancient Celtic symbol of nobility of character as well as of birth. The thistle has special significance in Elizabethan embroidery as it has been the national emblem of Scotland since the reign of Alexander III (1249-1286).

Through much of her reign, Elizabeth I was troubled by the presence in England of Mary, Queen of Scots. Mary had been forced to abdicate her throne in 1567 and she fled to England seeking the protection of her father's cousin, Elizabeth. The English queen was wary of her Scottish counterpart as many Catholics still believed that Mary was the rightful queen of England, Elizabeth having been declared illegitimate upon the execution of her mother, Anne Boleyn, in 1536. Elizabeth solved the problem by having Mary executed in 1587.

Mary was also a keen embroiderer and pieces of her work use the thistle to symbolise her ties with Scotland. In England, it was a popular motif in both blackwork and coloured silk embroidery.

Another popular plant was St. Benedict's thistle or *Cnicus Benedictus*. In Elizabethan times every cottage gardener grew this plant as it was a popular vegetable. The thistle root was boiled and eaten, and the heads cooked like artichokes. Today, this thistle is an effective bitter tonic that stimulates the appetite and strengthens the digestive system.

The entry in Gerard's Herball or General Historie of Plantes, 1633 reads:

"Carduus. Of Thistle vpon Thistle, and diuers other Wilde Thistles. [Dioscorides] affirmeth also, that the herbe being as yet greene and tender is vsed to be eaten among other herbes after the manner of Asparagus."

THREADS

Wool

A = 1311 med grape
B = A245 dk olive green
C = 1643 khaki green
D = 1644 lt khaki green
E = 1652 olive green
F = 1692 med loden green
G = 1695 vy lt loden green
H = 1726 vy lt autumn yellow
I = A472 vy lt autumn yellow
J = 1750 vy dk old gold

Silk

A = 1343 Parma violet
B = 3736 dk khaki green
C = 3733 lt khaki green
D = 3713 lt grey-green
E = 2144 med grape green
F = 2115 med pistachio
G = 2131 vy lt grass green
H = 2514 copper yellow
I = 2543 corn
J = 524 golden olive

Primrose & Thistle

THIS DESIGN USES

French knot • Long and short stitch • Outline stitch
Satin stitch • Satin stitch padding • Split stitch • Stem stitch
Straight stitch • Trellis couching

using **H**, at the base of each petal of the full face flowers. Using two strands of **D**, work a French knot at the centre of these two flowers. Outline the receptacles and unopened bud in split stitch using **E**. Fill the shapes with satin stitch in the same colour and work straight stitch highlights using **F** (diag 1).

Thistle

Stems

Embroider the thistle stems in stem stitch using **B**.

Leaf

Outline the leaf in split stitch using **D**. Fill the leaf with long and short stitch using **C** and **D**. Stitch the centre vein in stem stitch using **B**.

Flowers

Outline the receptacles in split stitch using **D**. Fill the shapes with satin stitch padding and cover with satin stitch using the same colour. Work trellis couching over the shapes using **C** for both trellis and couching (diag 2).

Embroider the flower heads in straight stitch and long and short stitch using **A**.

Curlicues

Using **J**, stitch each curl using one row of stem stitch and one row of outline stitch for the wool and one row of outline or stem stitch for the silk.

ORDER OF WORK

All embroidery is worked with one strand of thread unless specified.

Main stem

Using **B**, work the main stem in stem stitch, beginning below the upper primrose. Stitch down the stem, around the curving tip and back to the starting point.

Primrose

Stems

Stitch the remaining stems and the upper curl in stem stitch using **B**.

Leaves

Outline the small leaf near the base of the stem and the large upper leaf in split stitch using **E**. Fill the lower leaf with satin stitch in the same colour and work a stem stitch vein using **F**. Using **E** and **F**, fill the upper leaf with long and short stitch.

Flowers and buds

Outline the petals of all the flowers in split stitch using **G**. Fill each petal on the full face flowers with satin stitch padding and cover with satin stitch using the same colour. Pad the front petal on the side view flower with satin stitch padding. Using **G**, cover the petal with satin stitch and stitch the remaining petals on this flower and the partially opened flower in satin stitch. Using **I** and referring to the photograph for colour placement, work several straight stitches at the base of the petals. Work a single straight stitch,

TRELLIS COUCHING

An open, decorative filling, trellis couching can be worked over a base of stitches or straight onto the fabric.

Work the foundation layer of stitches.

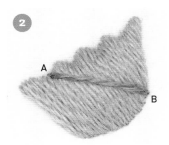

Bring the thread to the front at A. Take it to the back at B.

Bring the thread to the front at C and work a second straight stitch parallel to the first.

Continue working evenly spaced straight stitches. To position the stitch, lay the thread across the shape before taking the needle to the back.

Bring the thread to the front at D and work a straight stitch across the first layer.

Stitch the remaining straight stitches.

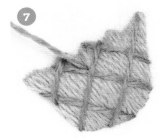

Bring the couching thread to the surface just above a thread intersection.

Work a small straight stitch over the two threads.

Continue in this manner until all intersections are couched.

PRIMROSE MOTIF

THIS DESIGN USES

French knot • Outline stitch • Satin stitch • Satin stitch padding
Stem stitch • Straight stitch

THREADS

Wool

A = 1750 vy dk old gold
B = 1692 med loden green
C = 1695 vy lt loden green
D = 1652 olive green
E = A472 vy lt autumn yellow
F = 1726 vy lt autumn yellow
G = 1644 lt khaki green
H = A245 dk olive green

Silk

A = 524 golden olive
B = 2115 med pistachio
C = 2131 vy lt grass green
D = 2144 med grape green
E = 2543 corn
F = 2514 copper yellow
G = 3713 lt grey-green
H = 3736 dk khaki green

ORDER OF WORK

All embroidery is worked with one strand of thread unless specified.

Primrose

Stem

Stitch the stem with stem stitch using **H**.

Leaf

Outline the leaf with split stitch and cover each half with angled satin stitch using **D**. Work the vein with stem stitch using **B**.

Flower

Outline each petal with split stitch and fill with satin stitch padding using **C**. Cover each petal with satin stitch using the same thread. Using **E**, work several straight stitches into the base of each petal and a single straight stitch at the centre using **F**. Work a French knot at the centre using two strands of **G**.

Curlicue

Stitch the curlicue with outline stitch using **A**.

Acorn & Gillyflower

IMMORTALITY + DIGNITY

Acorn

QUERCUS ROBUR

THE acorn motif appears throughout the history of embroidery. It reached its height of popularity during the Elizabethan period, where it was used in blackwork, crewelwork and polychrome silk embroidery.

The acorn is the familiar fruit or nut of the English oak, a large, deciduous tree with very decorative lobed leaves. As a building timber, oak was greatly prized and was used to construct the framework for houses, farm buildings, inns and theatres, and the roof beams for churches, cathedrals and castle halls. Quarter-sawn boards of oak were used to panel the debating chamber of the House of Commons in London. The timber was also used to construct fine furniture.

Oak bark is rich in tannin and was used for tanning leather and oak galls have been used for centuries to make manuscript ink.

Those of lesser means had a different use as the following passage shows.

"A Description of Elizabethan England"

"The bread throughout the land is made of such grain as the soil yieldeth; nevertheless the gentility commonly provide themselves sufficiently of wheat for their own tables, whilst their household and poor neighbours in some shires are forced to content themselves with rye, or barley, yea, and in time of dearth, many with bread made either of beans, peas, or oats, or of altogether and some acorns among, of which scourge the poorest do soonest taste, sith they are least able to provide themselves of better."

WILLIAM HARRISON, 1577

Gillyflower

DIANTHUS CAROPHYLLUS

GILLYFLOWER was a term used in Elizabethan times to describe a number of different scented flowering plants, the carnation, pink, stock or wallflower.

In the context of Elizabethan embroidery, the gillyflower was the carnation and was an emblem of love and affection.

Its popularity was second only to the beloved rose, both as a garden plant and motif for embroidery.

Carnations are edible flowers with a spicy, clove-like scent and are native to regions of the Mediterranean. They are thought to have been introduced to England by the Romans in 55BC.

The entry in Gerard's Herball or General Historie of Plantes, 1633 reads:

"Caryophyllus. Pinks or wilde Gillofloures. The conserue made of the floures of the Cloue Gillofloure and sugar, is exceeding cordial, and wonderfully aboue measure doth comfort the heart, being eaten now and then.

John Parkinson, Paradisus in Sole

"But what shall I say to the Queen of delight and of flowers, Carnations and Gilloflowers, whose bravery, variety and sweete smell joyned together, tyeth every ones affection with great earnestness, both to like them and to have them?"

"I take this goodly great old English Carnation, as a precedent for the description of all the rest, which for his beauty and stateliness is worthy of prime place."

PARADISUS TERRESTRIS, 1629

Acorn &
Gillyflower

THIS DESIGN USES

Blanket stitch • Couching • French knot • Long and short stitch
Outline stitch • Satin stitch • Satin stitch padding • Split stitch
Stem stitch • Straight stitch

THREADS

Wool

A = 1451 dk khaki brown
B = 1642 med khaki green
C = 1644 lt khaki green
D = 1651 dk olive green
E = 1730 vy dk honey gold
F = 1750 vy dk old gold
G = 1752 med old gold
H = A754 rose pink
I = A942 vy lt bright rose pink
J = 1948 ultra vy lt cranberry

Silk

A = 3836 vy dk mouse
B = 3734 khaki green
C = 3713 lt grey-green
D = 516 dk leaf green
E = 2246 vy dk colonial gold
F = 524 golden olive
G = 2234 bronze
H = 2933 carnation
I = 2931 vy lt carnation
J = 4147 ultra lt China rose

At the centre of the open-face flower, work long and short stitch using **I** to form the flower centre. Fill each petal of the flower bud with close blanket stitch using **H**, ensuring that the beaded edge is at the top of the petals. Outline the flower and bud receptacles with split stitch using **C**. Fill with satin stitch padding and cover with satin stitch using the same colour. Using **A**, work straight stitches to outline each section, couching them in place with the same thread as required (diag 1).

Acorn

Stems

Work the stems to the leaves and nuts in stem stitch using **B**.

Leaves

Outline each leaf with split stitch using **D**. Pad each side with straight stitch using the same colour. Work angled satin stitch over each leaf, beginning at the base on one side. Work up and around the tip and back to the base.

Acorns

Outline the cap of each acorn in split stitch using **E**. Fill with satin stitch padding and cover with satin stitch using the same colour. Work a layer of French knots over the satin stitch using **E**.

Outline the nut of each acorn in split stitch using **G**. Fill with satin stitch padding and cover with satin stitch using **G**. Work a tiny straight stitch at the tip of each nut using **E**.

Curlicues

Using **F**, stitch each curl using one row of stem stitch and one row of outline stitch for the wool and one row of outline or stem stitch for the silk.

ORDER OF WORK

All embroidery is worked with one strand of thread.

Main stem

Using **B**, work the main stem in stem stitch, beginning below the open flower. Stitch down around the curving tip and back to the flower.

Gillyflower

Stems

Stitch the remaining flower stems in stem stitch using **B**.

Leaves

Using **C**, outline each leaf in split stitch then fill the shape with rows of split stitch in the same colour. Beginning at the stem, work each leaf stem in stem stitch, using **B**, continuing in split stitch to the tip of the leaf for the centre vein.

Flowers and bud

Using **H**, outline the petals of the open face and two side view flowers with split stitch. Using the same colour, work long and short stitch halfway down each petal. Fill the remaining space on each petal with long and short stitch using **J**.

ACORN

The raised texture of the acorns is created with several layers of satin stitch padding.

Outline the cap in split stitch.

Fill with satin stitch padding and cover with satin stitch.

Work French knots over the satin stitch, beginning around the edge.

Outline the nut in split stitch.

Fill with satin stitch padding and cover with satin stitch.

Work a small straight stitch at the tip of the acorn.

ACORN MOTIF

THREADS

Wool

A = 1651 dk olive green
B = 1730 vy dk honey gold
C = 1750 vy dk old gold
D = 1752 med old gold

Silk

A = 516 dk leaf-green
B = 2246 vy dk colonial gold
C = 3734 khaki green
D = 2234 bronze

ORDER OF WORK

All embroidery is worked with one strand of thread.

Stem

Using **C**, work the stem in outline and/or stem stitch. Stitch the stem to the acorns in stem stitch using the same colour.

Acorns

Outline the cap of each acorn in split stitch using **B**. Fill with satin stitch padding and cover with satin stitch using the same colour. Work a layer of French knots over the satin stitch using **B**.

Outline the nut of each acorn in split stitch using **D**. Fill with satin stitch padding and cover with satin stitch using **D**. Work a tiny straight stitch at the tip of each acorn using **B**.

Leaf

Using **A**, outline the leaf in split stitch, then cover with satin stitch.

THIS DESIGN USES

French knot • Outline stitch • Satin stitch • Satin stitch padding
Split stitch • Stem stitch • Straight stitch

GILLYFLOWER MOTIF

THIS DESIGN USES

Couching • Outline stitch • Satin stitch • Satin stitch padding
• Split stitch • Stem stitch • Straight stitch

THREADS

Wool

A = 1451 dk khaki brown
B = A244 med olive green
C = 1643 khaki green
D = 1694 lt loden green
E = 1750 vy dk old gold
F = A754 rose pink
G = 1948 ultra vy lt cranberry

Silk

A = 3836 vy dk mouse
B = 3735 med khaki green
C = 3733 lt khaki green
D = 2132 lt grass green
E = 524 golden olive
F = 2933 carnation
G = 4147 ultra lt China rose

ORDER OF WORK

All embroidery is worked with one strand of thread.

Stem

Using **E**, work the stem in outline and/or stem stitch. Work the stem to the leaf in stem stitch using the same colour.

Flower

Using **F**, outline the petals with split stitch. Using the same colour, work long and short stitch halfway down the shape. Fill the remaining space with long and short stitch using **G**. Using **D**, outline the receptacle in split stitch. Fill with satin stitch padding and cover with satin stitch. Using **A**, work straight stitches to outline each section, couching them in place with the same thread as required.

Leaf

Outline the leaf in split stitch using **C**. Fill the shape with rows of split stitch in the same colour. Work the leaf vein in split stitch using **B**.

Heartsease & Eglantine

—— THOUGHTS + SIMPLICITY ——

Heartsease

VIOLA TRICOLOR

HEARTSEASE is an edible wild pansy and has been used for centuries by herbalists to treat respiratory complaints, skin diseases and arthritis.

A common wildflower that grows throughout Europe, it is a small plant with a creeping habit and its natural habitat is grassland where it prefers partial shade.

The flowers are followed by large seedpods and it self-seeds very easily, perhaps a reason for its alternative name of Johnny Jump Up. It flowers from spring through summer and the bright little faces are a delight to see in the garden.

It is from this dainty little purple and yellow flower that modern pansy hybrids are derived.

Heartsease was a flower significant to Elizabeth I as she chose heartsease to ornament two embroidered bindings she stitched as a child. One was made as a gift for her stepmother, Queen Katherine Parr in 1544 and another for her father in 1545.

Heart's ease! one could look for half a day
Upon this flower, and shape in fancy out
Full twenty different tales of love and sorrow,
That gave this gentle name.

HEART'S EASE, MARY HOWITT

Eglantine

ROSA EGLANTERIA

WITHOUT doubt, the rose was the most popular motif used by the Elizabethans in their embroidery. National emblem of England, the rose is most significant in Elizabethan times in two forms, eglantine and the Tudor rose.

Also known as sweet briar, eglantine was a favourite flower of Elizabeth I. A deciduous shrub, it grows 2–3m (6–10 ft) high and the stems bear hooked thorns. The foliage smells strongly of apples and the five-petalled flowers are pink with a white base. It produces oblong red hips and is spread by birds that eat the seeds. Extremely hardy, this rose will survive neglect and in some countries has become a weed.

What's in a name? That which we call a rose.
By any other name would smell as sweet.

ROMEO AND JULIET, ACT II SCENE II
WILLIAM SHAKESPEARE, 1597

Heartsease
& Eglantine

THREADS

Wool

A = 1311 med grape
B = 1451 dk khaki brown
C = 1642 med khaki green
D = 1643 khaki green
E = 1651 dk olive green
F = 1652 olive green
G = 1726 vy lt autumn yellow
H = 1731 dk honey gold
I = 1733 honey gold
J = 1750 vy dk old gold
K = 1831 dk bittersweet
L = A754 rose pink
M = 1933 rusty rose
N = A942 vy lt bright rose pink

Silk

A = 1343 Parma violet
B = 3837 vy dk mouse
C = 3734 khaki green
D = 3733 lt khaki green
E = 516 dk leaf green
F = 2144 med grape green
G = 2514 copper yellow
H = 2245 dk colonial gold
I = 2515 med copper yellow
J = 524 golden olive
K = 2636 dk terracotta
L = 2933 carnation
M = 2932 lt carnation
N = 2931 vy lt carnation

THIS DESIGN USES

Blanket stitch • Detached chain • French knot • Long and short stitch
Outline stitch • Satin stitch • Satin stitch padding • Split stitch
Stem stitch • Straight stitch

ORDER OF WORK

All embroidery is worked with one strand of thread unless specified.

Main stem

Using **H**, work the main stem in stem stitch, beginning below the eglantine flower. Stitch down the stem, around the curving tip and back to the starting point.

Heartsease

Stems

Stitch the flower and bud stems in outline stitch using **F**.

Leaves

Using **F**, work close blanket stitch around each leaf, beginning with a detached chain (diag 1).

Work each centre vein using **E**, beginning at the stem and working almost to the tip of the leaf in stem stitch. Embroider straight stitch veins along each side of the leaf in the same colour.

Flowers

Using **I**, outline the lower petals with split stitch. Fill each petal with satin stitch padding and cover with satin stitch, using the same colour. Using **G**, work several straight stitches from the centre onto each petal of the open flowers. Cut a 25cm (10") length of **B**. Carefully separate the two plies that make up the strand. Thread one into the needle and work 3–5 straight stitches over the previously worked stitches, twisting the thread tightly to create a narrow stitch.

Using **A**, outline the upper petals with split stitch. Fill each petal with satin stitch padding and cover with satin

stitch, using the same colour. Embroider a French knot at the centre of each open flower, using two strands of **D**. Work a straight stitch on each side of the French knot, beginning each at the same point just above the centre using **B** (diag 2).

Embroider the sepals on the partially opened flower in close blanket stitch using **F**, keeping the beaded edge towards the flower petals.

Eglantine

Stems

Work the stems to the hips in stem stitch using **H** and the stem to the bud using **E**.

Leaves

Outline each leaf with split stitch using **D**. Fill with long and short stitch using **D** and **C**. Using **C**, stitch the centre vein in outline stitch beginning at the stem.

Flower and bud

Outline the petals in split stitch using **N**. Fill each petal with rows of long and short stitch, beginning with **N** at the outer edge, changing to **M** then **L**. Outline the centre in split stitch using **G**. Fill the centre with satin stitch padding and cover with satin stitch in the same colour. Scatter French knots around the centre and the base of the petals using **G**. Embroider a straight stitch surrounded by a detached chain at the intersection of each petal using **C**.

Outline the bud with split stitch using **C**. Fill with satin stitch padding and cover with satin stitch in the same colour. Work a wedge of straight stitches at the centre top using **L**. Using the photograph as a guide, work straight stitches along each side and at the tip of the bud using **C**. Stitch the receptacle at the base of the bud in satin stitch with the same colour.

Hips

Outline each hip in split stitch using **K**. Fill with satin stitch padding and cover with satin stitch using the same colour. Work the sepals in straight stitch using **B**.

Curlicues

Using **J**, embroider each curl with one row of stem stitch and one row of outline stitch for the wool and one row of outline or stem stitch for the silk.

BLANKET STITCH LEAF

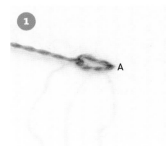

Bring the thread to the front at A and work a detached chain, without anchoring the stitch.

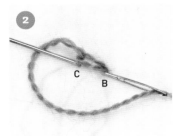

Take the needle to the back at B and emerge at C. Ensure that the thread is under the needle.

Pull the thread through.

Continue working blanket stitches along one side of the leaf.

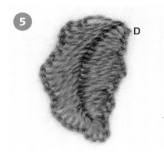

Fan the stitches around the tip and work along the remaining side. Take the thread to the back at D and secure.

Veins. Bring the thread to the surface at the main stem.

Work stem stitch almost to the tip of the leaf.

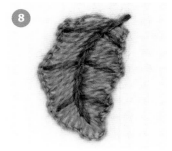

Work straight stitch veins across each side of the leaf.

ROSEHIP MOTIF

THIS DESIGN USES

Outline stitch • Satin stitch • Satin stitch padding
Split stitch • Stem stitch • Straight stitch

THREADS

Wool

A = 1451 dk khaki brown
B = 1642 med khaki green
C = 1643 khaki green
D = 1731 dk honey gold
E = 1750 dk old gold
F = 1831 dk bittersweet

Silk

A = 3836 vy dk mouse
B = 3734 khaki green
C = 3733 lt khaki green
D = 2245 dk colonial gold
E = 524 golden olive
F = 2636 dk terracotta

ORDER OF WORK

All embroidery is worked with one strand of thread.

Stem

Using **E**, work the stem in outline and/or stem stitch. Work the stems to the leaf and hips in stem stitch using **D**.

Hips

Using **F**, outline the hips in split stitch. Fill the shapes with satin stitch padding and cover with satin stitch. Work the sepals in straight stitch using **A**.

Leaves

Using **C**, outline the leaves in split stitch. Fill each leaf with long and short stitch using **B** and **C**. Stitch the centre vein in stem stitch using **B**.

HEARTSEASE MOTIF

THIS DESIGN USES

Blanket stitch • Detached chain • French knot • Outline stitch
Satin stitch • Satin stitch padding • Split stitch • Stem stitch
Straight stitch

THREADS

Wool

A = 1311 med grape
B = 1450 vy dk khaki brown
C = 1652 olive green
D = 1694 lt loden green
E = 1726 vy lt autumn yellow
F = 1750 vy dk old gold

Silk

A = 1343 Parma violet
B = 4536 vy dk beige
C = 2144 med grape green
D = 2132 lt grass green
E = 2514 copper yellow
F = 524 golden olive

ORDER OF WORK

All embroidery is worked with one strand of thread unless specified.

Stem

Using **F**, work the stem in outline and/or stem stitch. Work the stem to the leaf in stem stitch using the same colour. Embroider the stems to the pansy and bud in outline stitch using **C**.

Flower and bud

Using **E**, outline the lower petals with split stitch. Fill the petals with satin stitch padding and cover with satin stitch. Work the upper petals in the same manner using **A**. Cut a 25cm (10") length of **B**. Carefully separate the two plies that make up the strand. Thread one into the needle and work 3–5 straight stitches over the previously worked stitches on the open flower, twisting the thread tightly to create a narrow stitch.

Using two strands of **D**, work a French knot at the centre of the pansy. Using **B**, stitch a detached chain around the French knot. Embroider the sepals on the bud in straight stitch using **C** and the receptacle in close blanket stitch in the same colour.

Leaves

Using **C**, stitch each leaf in close blanket stitch, beginning with a detached chain. Work the centre vein in the same colour, using outline stitch for the left-hand leaf and stem stitch for the right-hand leaf.

Cornflower
& Strawberry

—— DELICACY + RIGHTEOUSNESS ——

Cornflower

CENTAUREA CYANUS

THE bright blue cornflower is an annual native to Europe. Like the red poppy, it originally grew as a weed in fields of grain crops. It grows to around 90cm (3ft) in height and has grey-ish-green foliage. The flowers are a particularly intense blue and have a few large spreading florets surrounding a central cluster of small disc florets.

It readily self seeds and is particularly pretty when planted amongst soft pink roses and white daisies.

Both its colour and flower form made it of interest to the Elizabethan embroiderer. It was used as a motif in blackwork and coloured silk embroidery.

A decoction of the flowers is very effective in treating conjunctivitis.

Strawberry

FRAGARIA VESCA

THE strawberry of Elizabethan times was not the large, lush fruit that we enjoy today. Theirs was a much smaller, intensely flavoured berry that grew wild along roadsides and embankments and was commonly referred to as the woodland strawberry. Brought into the home garden, it was used for food and was a favourite of embroiderers as it displayed a pleasing colour scheme with the plants carrying flowers and ripe berries at the same time.

Favourite recipes included strawberry pies and tarts, cordials, preserves and strawberry butters.

This dainty wild strawberry is still available as a garden plant and is grown in commercial quantities for use in jams, sauces, liqueurs, cosmetics and alternative medicines.

Cultivated by the Romans as early as 200BC, strawberries were thought to be an aphrodisiac and in mediaeval times, a soup of strawberries, sour cream and borage was served to newlyweds at the wedding breakfast.

Early uses of strawberries were in medicine and not as a food, and in the 12th century, Saint Hildegard von Bingen pronounced strawberries unfit to eat because they may have been contaminated by snakes and toads due to the fact that they were grown close to the ground.

A Tarte of Strawberries from A Proper Newe Booke

Take and strain them with the yolks of four eggs, and a little white bread grated, then season it up with sugar and sweet butter and so bake it.

Cornflower
& Strawberry

THIS DESIGN USES

Detached Chain • Fly stitch • French knot • Outline stitch
Satin stitch • Satin stitch padding • Split stitch • Stem stitch
Straight stitch • Trellis couching

THREADS

Wool

A = 1263 cream
B = 1560 dk glacier
C = A743 lt bright China blue
D = 1570 navy blue
E = 1643 khaki green
F = 1644 lt khaki green
G = A256 ultra dk grass green
H = 1651 dk olive green
I = 1726 vy lt autumn yellow
J = 1730 vy dk honey gold
K = 1750 vy dk old gold
L = 1840 vy dk salmon
M = 1841 dk salmon
N = 1902 med American red

Silk

A = 4102 cream
B = 4914 med hyacinth
C = 1421 vy lt marine blue
D = 1426 dk marine blue
E = 3733 lt khaki green
F = 3713 lt grey-green
G = 2145 dk grape green
H = 516 dk leaf green
I = 2514 copper yellow
J = 2246 vy dk colonial gold
K = 524 golden olive
L = 944 med garnet
M = 926 vy dk peony
N = 3015 dk geranium

Pad each side with straight stitch using the same colour. Work angled satin stitch over each leaf using **G**. Begin at the base on one side and work up, around the tip and back to the base. Stitch the centre veins in stem stitch using **G**, working each from the main stem, towards the tip.

Flowers and bud

Using **A**, outline the petals in split stitch. Fill each petal with satin stitch padding and cover with satin stitch using the same colour. Using **F**, work a straight stitch between each petal and three straight stitches at the base of each petal of the open flower. Embroider a cluster of French knots at the centre of the open flower using **I**.

Using **G**, work the sepals on the bud in straight stitch. Work the sepal tips between the petals of the open flower in detached chain and under the side view flower in detached chain and split stitch (diag 1).

ORDER OF WORK

All embroidery is worked with one strand of thread unless specified.

Main stem

Using **J**, work the main stem in stem stitch, beginning below the open cornflower. Stitch down the stem, around the curving tip and back to the starting point.

Cornflower

Stems

Stitch the stems to the side view flower and bud in stem stitch using **J**.

Leaves

Using **E**, outline each leaf with split stitch. Fill the shape with rows of split stitch in the same colour.

Flowers and bud

Using **E**, outline the receptacles with

split stitch. Fill each one with satin stitch padding and cover with satin stitch using the same colour. Work trellis couching over the shapes using **F** for the straight stitches and **J** for the small couching stitch. Beginning with **B**, work fly stitch to create the flower petals. Embroider a second layer of fly stitch using **C**. Referring to the photograph, work small straight stitches using **D** at the centre of the open flower and amongst the petals of the side view flower. Using **N**, scatter small straight stitches onto both flowers. Stitch the bud petals in straight stitch using **B**.

Strawberry

Stems

Work the stems to the berries and flowers in stem stitch using **J**.

Leaves

Using **G**, outline each leaf in split stitch.

Berries

Using **L**, outline the three large berries in split stitch. Fill each one with satin stitch padding and cover with satin stitch. Repeat for the small berry using **F**. Work trellis couching over the large berries, using **M** for the straight stitches and **K** for the small couching stitches. Repeat for the small berry, using **E** for the straight stitches and **K** for the small couching stitches. Embroider the berry sepals in detached chain using two strands of **H**.

Curlicues

Using **K**, embroider each curl using one row of stem stitch and one row of outline stitch for the wool and one row of outline or stem stitch for the silk.

SATIN STITCH PADDING

Perfect for creating raised, domed shapes, this layered form of padding is also a great way to practise satin stitch.

Outline the shape in split stitch.

Work the first layer of padding.

Stitch the second layer at right angles to the first, making the stitches slightly longer.

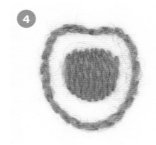

Work a third layer, again at right angles to the previous layer and slightly larger.

Continue working layers of padding until the shape is full. Ensure that the last layer is at a right angle to the final row of satin stitches.

Beginning at the centre of the shape, work satin stitch over one half.

Return to the centre and stitch the remaining half of the shape with satin stitch.

CORNFLOWER MOTIF

THIS DESIGN USES

Fly stitch • Outline stitch • Satin stitch • Satin stitch padding
Split stitch • Stem stitch • Straight stitch • Trellis couching

THREADS

Wool

A = 1560 dk glacier
B = A743 lt bright China blue
C = 1570 navy blue
D = A244 med olive green
E = 1643 khaki green
F = 1730 vy dk honey gold
G = 1750 vy dk old gold
H = 1902 med American red

Silk

A = 4914 med hyacinth
B = 1421 vy lt marine blue
C = 1426 dk marine blue
D = 3735 med khaki green
E = 3733 lt khaki green
F = 2246 vy dk colonial gold
G = 524 golden olive
H = 3015 dk geranium

ORDER OF WORK

All embroidery is worked with one strand of thread.

Stem

Using **G**, work the stem in outline and/or stem stitch. Work the stem to the leaf in stem stitch using the same colour.

Flower

Using **E**, outline the receptacle with split stitch. Fill with satin stitch padding and cover with satin stitch using the same colour. Work trellis couching over the shape using **D** for the straight stitches and **F** for the small couching stitches. Beginning with **A**, work fly stitches to create the flower petals. Embroider a second layer of fly stitches using **B**. Using the photograph as a guide, scatter small straight stitches using **C** and **H** over the flower.

Leaf

Using **E**, outline the leaf in split stitch. Fill with rows of split stitch using the same colour.

STRAWBERRY MOTIF

THIS DESIGN USES

Detached chain • Outline stitch • Satin stitch • Satin stitch padding
Split stitch • Stem stitch • Straight stitch • Trellis couching

THREADS

Wool

A = A256 ultra dk grass green
B = 1651 dk olive green
C = 1750 vy dk old gold
D = 1840 vy dk salmon
E = 1841 dk salmon

Silk

A = 2145 dk grape green
B = 516 dk leaf green
C = 524 golden olive
D = 944 med garnet
E = 926 vy dk peony
F = 2246 vy dk colonial gold

ORDER OF WORK

All embroidery is worked with one strand of thread.

Stem

Using **C** for the wool and **F** for the silk, work the stem in outline and/or stem stitch. Work the stem to the berry in stem stitch using the same colour.

Berry

Using **D**, outline the berry in split stitch. Fill with satin stitch padding and cover with satin stitch using the same colour. Work trellis couching over the shape, using **E** for the straight stitches and **C** for the couching. Work detached chain at the top of the berry using **B**.

Leaf

Using **A**, outline the leaf in split stitch, pad with straight stitch then cover with satin stitch.

Pomegranate & Cranesbill

Pomegranate

PUNICA GRANATUM

THE pomegranate is native to Southwest Asia. It has been cultivated and naturalised over the entire Mediterranean and Caucasus since ancient times. It was introduced to England in the 16th century by John Tradescant the Elder but the cold climate severely inhibited its fruiting.

The pomegranate grows as a deciduous shrub or small tree and has bright vermillion flowers that develop into large orange-red globular fruits. This fruit has a tough, leathery skin that splits open to reveal jewel-like seeds or arils, covered in a juicy red pulp. The plant can have flowers and fruit at the same time, making it a very attractive addition to the garden.

The pomegranate was the symbol of Katherine of Aragon, first wife of Henry VIII.

Pomegranate juice is high in vitamin C, B5, potassium and anti-oxidants. It reduces blood pressure and heart disease risk factors.

The pomegranate symbol can be found in many cultures, as a holy symbol or representing fertility, abundance and good luck. It was a very popular blackwork motif in Elizabethan embroidery.

The name is derived from the Latin *pomum* (apple) and *granatus* (seeded). In French it is known as 'la grenade' and is used to make a pomegranate syrup called 'grenadine'.

The entry in Gerard's Herball or General Historie of Plantes 1633 reads:

"Malus Granata, siue Punica. Of the Pomegranat tree. As there be sundry sorts of Apples, Peares, Plums, and such like fruits, so there are two sorts of Pomegranates, the garden and the wilde... the fruit of the garden Pomegranat is of three sorts; one hauing a soure iuyce or liquor; another hauing a very sweet and pleasant liquor, and the third the taste of wine... The iuicie grains of the Pomegranate are good to be eaten, hauing in them a meetly good iuice: they are wholesome for the stomacke..."

Cranesbill

GERANIUM PRATENSE

CRANESBILL is the common name for hundreds of species of flowering geraniums that are found throughout temperate regions, particularly the eastern part of the Mediterranean.

The name comes from the resemblance of the long, unopened seed pod to the bill of a crane. When ripe, this pod springs open to fling the seeds as far as possible.

Geraniums are hardy garden plants that will tolerate most soils and can be struck from cuttings or grown from seed.

The Elizabethans were familiar with the blue-flowered meadow cranesbill, native to England and a popular choice for the home garden. It was also known under a variety of other names such as crowfoot cranesbill, bassinets, loving Andrews and *gratia dei* (grace of God). This variety of geranium grows well on chalky or limey soils and in the wild, grows on banks or by the roadside. It can be invasive so it is best grown in an area of wild garden.

This was another of the meadow plants, like poppies and cornflowers, that the Elizabethans found so attractive, bringing them into their gardens for cultivation.

Cranesbills can be grown from the seeds that spring from the elongated pods. Plant them in friable soil or seed raising mix then transfer into the ground or a pot once the plants are 5cm (2") high. Make sure that they are positioned in a sunny spot and have adequate moisture until they are well established. Alternatively, cuttings can be used to propagate plants. Dip the cut end into hormone rooting powder and place several cuttings into a pot until they take root. Transfer into the garden or individual pots.

Pomegranate
& Cranesbill

THREADS

Wool

A = 1263 cream
B = 1311 med grape
C = 1450 vy dk khaki brown
D = A745 med bright China blue
E = 1570 navy blue
F = 1642 med khaki green
G = 1643 khaki green
H = 1644 lt khaki green
I = A256 ultra dk grass green
J = 1651 dk olive green
K = 1652 olive green
L = 1730 vy dk honey gold
M = 1750 vy dk old gold
N = 1831 dk bittersweet
O = 1840 vy dk salmon
P = 1841 dk salmon

Silk

A = 4102 cream
B = 1343 Parma violet
C = 4536 vy dk beige
D = 1422 lt marine blue
E = 1426 dk marine blue
F = 3734 khaki green
G = 3733 lt khaki green
H = 3713 lt grey-green
I = 2145 dk grape green
J = 516 dk leaf green
K = 2144 med grape green
L = 2246 vy dk colonial gold
M = 524 golden olive
N = 2636 dk terracotta
O = 944 med garnet
P = 926 vy dk peony

THIS DESIGN USES

Fly stitch • French knot • Outline stitch • Long and short stitch
Satin stitch • Satin stitch padding • Split stitch • Stem stitch
Straight stitch • Trellis couching

ORDER OF WORK

All embroidery is worked with one strand of thread.

Main stem

Using **C**, work the main stem in stem stitch, beginning at the small pomegranate. Stitch down around the curving tip and back to the starting point. Stitch the curling stem in stem stitch using the same thread.

Pomegranate

Stems

Stitch the stems to the fruit and centre leaf in stem stitch using **C**.

Leaves

Using **G**, outline each leaf with split stitch. Fill the shape with rows of split stitch in the same colour. Stitch the centre vein in outline stitch using **F**.

Fruit

Using **N**, outline the pomegranates with split stitch, including the opening on the large fruit. Using the photograph as a guide to colour placement, work long and short stitch to fill the shapes using **N**, **O**, **P**, **L** and **M**. Using **L**, work fly stitch around the lower edges (diag 1).

Using **C**, work split stitch around the edge of the small pomegranate where it overlaps the large one. Fill the centre of the large fruit with long and short stitch

using **A**. Work trellis couching using **O** and **P** for the long straight stitches and **O** for the small couching stitches.

Cranesbill

Stems

Using **K**, work the stems to the flowers and seed pods in stem stitch.

Leaves

Referring to the photograph for colour placement, work the leaves in satin stitch and straight stitch using **I** and **J**.

Flowers

Using **D**, outline all flower petals in split stitch. Fill each petal with satin stitch padding and cover with satin stitch using the same colour. Using **B**, embroider straight stitches, separating the petals on each flower.

Work several straight stitches, using **B**, onto the base of the petals on the partially opened flowers. Using **E**, fill the centres of the large flowers with French knots, sprinkling knots around the base of the petals. Outline the unopened buds and flower receptacles in split stitch using **K**. Pad with straight stitch then cover in satin stitch using the same colour. Using **J**, add straight stitches as indicated (diag 2).

Seed pods

Outline the base of each pod in split stitch using **H**. Pad each pod with straight stitches and cover with satin stitch in the same colour. Using **I** and **J**, embroider the sepals at the top of the seed pods in the same manner as the leaves.

Curlicues

Using **M**, stitch each curl using one row of stem stitch and one row of outline stitch for the wool and one row of outline or stem stitch for the silk.

CRANESBILL SEED POD

These long, narrow pods are padded with straight stitches then covered in satin stitch.

1 Outline the lower part of the pod with split stitch.

2 Pad the shape with straight stitch, working several layers on top of one another.

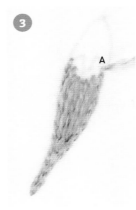

3 Bring the thread to the surface at A, just outside the split stitch line.

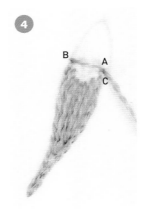

4 Take the thread to the back at B and emerge at C, just below A.

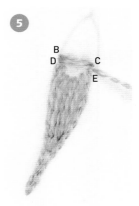

5 Take the thread to the back at D, just below B and emerge at E, just below C.

6 Continue working satin stitch in this manner to the end of the shape.

7 Work a layer of satin stitches for the sepals.

8 Work several straight stitches over the satin stitch using the darker colour.

CRANESBILL MOTIF

THIS DESIGN USES

French knot • Outline stitch • Satin stitch • Satin stitch padding
Split stitch • Stem stitch • Straight stitch

THREADS

Wool

A = 1311 med grape
B = A745 med bright China blue
C = 1570 navy blue
D = 1651 dk olive green
E = 1652 olive green
F = 1750 vy dk old gold

Silk

A = 1343 Parma violet
B = 1422 lt marine blue
C = 1426 dk marine blue
D = 516 dk leaf green
E = 2144 med grape green
F = 524 golden olive
G = 4536 vy dk beige

ORDER OF WORK

All embroidery is worked with one strand of thread.

Stem

Using **F** for the wool and **G** for the silk, work the stem in outline and/or stem stitch. Work the stem to the leaf in outline stitch using the same colour.

Flower

Using **B**, outline the petals in split stitch. Fill each petal with satin stitch padding and cover with satin stitch. Work a single straight stitch between each petal using **A**. Fill the centre of the flower with French knots and scatter knots over the base of each petal using **C**.

Leaves

Using **E**, stitch the leaves in straight stitch and add shading using **D**.

Peony & Buttercup

—— PROSPERITY + HAPPINESS ——

Peony

PAEONIA OFFICINALIS

THE peony takes its name from Paeon, a student of Ascelpius, the Greek god of medicine and healing.

Peonies have been cultivated in China for more than 2,000 years for both their beautiful flowers and their roots, which were used for food and medicine. The root was also used to treat a number of ailments including toothache, headache, seizures and the pain of childbirth.

Since ancient times, the peony has been regarded as a symbol of wealth, luck and happiness.

Brought to England by the Romans, peonies thrived in the English climate and became a popular garden plant. Their attractive foliage and large, blowsy flowers made a beautiful addition to both home and public gardens.

There are two quite distinct types of peony; the tree variety has woody stems and can grow up to 3m (10ft) in height while the herbaceous perennial only grows to around 1.5m (5ft) and disappears completely out of season. Both varieties have deeply lobed leaves and large, beautifully fragrant flowers that range in colour from white or yellow to red in single and double varieties.

They prefer rich, moist soil and will grow in semi-shade or sun. They are gross feeders and enjoy a regular application of manure or fertiliser.

A peony plant can live for up to fifty years so it is best to choose its planting position very carefully.

Buttercup

RANUNCULUS REPENS

THE buttercup is another of the native meadow plants that found its way onto embroideries in Elizabethan times. Native to England, the buttercup grows on open ground, in woods, hedgerows and in lawns. It can be incredibly invasive and difficult to control as it produces tiny bulbils that are difficult to eradicate completely.

Buttercups take their name from the belief that they could increase the amount of butter made from milk. This was because buttercups were prolific in rich pastures and the cows that fed on these pastures produced the best milk with the most cream. This actually had nothing to do with the buttercups as all Ranunculus species are poisonous to cattle and they will not eat them.

In Elizabethan times, the roots of this plant were used to treat piles (haemorrhoids), scrophula (a form of tuberculosis) and the plague.

Buttercups and daisies,
Oh the pretty flowers;
Coming ere the springtime,
To tell of sunny hours.

'BUTTERCUPS AND DAISIES'
MARY HOWITT (1799 - 1888)

THREADS

Wool

A = 1611 dk hunter green
B = 1612 med hunter green
C = A244 med olive green
D = 1692 med loden green
E = 1693 loden green
F = 1694 lt loden green
G = 1703 butterscotch
H = 1726 vy lt autumn yellow
I = 1750 vy dk old gold
J = 1902 med American red
K = 1920 vy dk wood rose
L = 1940 vy dk cranberry

Silk

A = 2135 dk grass green
B = 2134 med grass green
C = 3735 med khaki green
D = 2115 med pistachio
E = 2114 pistachio
F = 2132 lt grass green
G = 542 vy lt golden yellow
H = 2514 copper yellow
I = 524 golden olive
J = 3015 dk geranium
K = 4625 med plum
L = 1026 vy dk rose

Peony & Buttercup

THIS DESIGN USES

Bullion knot • Couching • French knot • Outline stitch
Long and short stitch • Satin stitch • Satin stitch padding
Split stitch • Stem stitch • Straight stitch

Using **L**, work several straight stitches over the lower half of the bud. Work the sepals over the leaf and bud in straight stitch using **B**.

Buttercup

Stems

Stitch the stems to the flowers with one or two rows of stem stitch using **B**.

Leaves

Using **B**, outline the small leaf on the main stem and the two upper leaves with split stitch. Work satin stitch over each leaf using **B**, adding partial split stitch outlines and straight stitch highlights using **A**.

Flowers and bud

Outline the petals in split stitch using **G**. Fill the bud and curled petal edges with satin stitch padding and cover with satin stitch in the same colour. Fill the remaining petals with long and short stitch in the same colour. Work straight stitches over the base of the bud and each petal using **H**. Fill the centre with satin stitch using **F**. Using **H**, work an arc of French knots along the upper edge of the centre and bullion knots along the lower edge (diag 1).

Using **B**, stitch several intersecting straight stitches across the centre and couch with a small straight stitch cross. Outline the calyx under the bud in split stitch using **F**. Pad with straight stitch and cover with satin stitches in the same colour. Using **B**, work several small straight stitches over the satin stitch as shown in the photograph.

Curlicues

Using **I**, stitch each curl with one row of stem stitch and one row of outline stitch for the wool and one row of outline or stem stitch for the silk.

ORDER OF WORK

All embroidery is worked with one strand of thread.

Main stem

Using **C**, work the stem in outline stitch, beginning below the open peony flower. Stitch down the stem, around the curving tip and back to the starting point.

Peony

Stems

Stitch the stem to the flower in outline stitch using **C**. Work the stem to the bud in the same colour with outline stitch once the large leaf is complete.

Leaves

Using **D**, outline each leaf with split stitch. Fill each section with rows of split stitch, except the underside section on the left-hand leaf. Fill this section with split stitch using **E**. Stitch the leaf veins in stem stitch using **K**.

Flower and bud

Outline each petal in split stitch using **J**. Pad the curled edges of the three front petals with satin stitch padding and cover with satin stitch using the same colour. Using **L**, fill the remainder of these petals with satin stitch. Work the remaining petals in long and short stitch, using **J** for the outer edge and **L** towards the centre. Fill the centre with satin stitch using **K** and work several straight stitches over the base of each back petal with the same colour. Using **H**, embroider French knots over the centre of the flower. Using **B**, outline the sepals in split stitch and cover with satin stitch using the same colour.

Outline the bud in split stitch using **J**. Fill the shape with satin stitch padding and cover with satin stitch in the same colour.

SPLIT STITCH LEAF

Work the split stitch outline carefully as this will help ensure that the edge of the leaf is smooth.

Bring the thread to the front and work a small straight stitch.

Bring the thread to the front through the centre of the previous stitch, splitting it.

Work a second straight stitch.

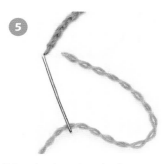

Continue working along the line. To stitch a sharp point, take the thread to the back at the leaf point.

Bring the thread to the front on the second side and take another stitch into the leaf point.

Bring the needle to the front through the centre of the previous stitch, splitting it.

Continue working around the edge of the leaf in this manner.

Continue working rows of split stitch inside the outline until the shape is filled.

Work the leaf veins in stem stitch, over the split stitch.

PEONY MOTIF

THIS DESIGN USES
Outline stitch • Satin stitch • Satin stitch padding
Split stitch • Stem stitch • Straight stitch

THREADS

Wool

A = 1612 med hunter green
B = 1692 med loden green
C = 1750 vy dk old gold
D = 1840 vy dk salmon
E = 1902 med American red
F = 1920 vy dk wood rose

Silk

A = 2134 med grass green
B = 2115 med pistachio
C = 524 golden olive
D = 944 med garnet
E = 3015 dk geranium
F = 4625 med plum

ORDER OF WORK

*All embroidery is worked with one strand
of thread.*

Stem

Using **C**, work the stem in outline and/or
stem stitch. Work the stem to the bud in
stem stitch using the same colour.

Bud

Using **E**, outline the bud in split stitch.
Fill with satin stitch padding and cover in
satin stitch using the same colour. Work
straight stitches into the base using **D**.
Work the sepals in straight stitch using **A**.

Leaf

Outline the leaf in split stitch using **B**.
Fill the shape with rows of split stitch.
Work the veins in stem stitch using **F**.

BUTTERCUP MOTIF

THIS DESIGN USES

Outline stitch • Satin stitch • Split stitch
Stem stitch • Straight stitch

THREADS

Wool

A = 1611 dk hunter green
B = 1612 med hunter green
C = 1694 lt loden green
D = 1703 butterscotch
E = 1726 vy lt autumn yellow
F = 1750 vy dk old gold

Silk

A = 2135 dk grass green
B = 2134 med grass green
C = 2132 lt grass green
D = 542 vy lt golden yellow
E = 2514 copper yellow
F = 524 golden olive
G = 3735 med khaki green

ORDER OF WORK

All embroidery is worked with one strand of thread.

Stem

Using **F** for the wool and **G** for the silk, work the stem in outline and/or stem stitch. Work the stem to the flower in outline stitch using the same colour.

Flowers

Using **E**, outline the flower in split stitch. Stitch the petals in satin stitch using **D** and **E** for the wool and **D**, **E** and **F** for the silk. Work the sepals in straight stitch, using **B** and **C**.

Leaf

Using **A** and **B**, stitch the leaf in satin stitch and straight stitch.

Pea & English Daisy

DEPARTURE + INNOCENCE

Pea

PISUM SATIVUM

PEAS have been grown as food since the early Bronze Age and are no longer known in their wild form. Use as a green table vegetable began in the Middle Ages and in Elizabethan times they were known as 'pease' and the pea pods as 'peasecods'. The first recorded detail of green peas was made in France in 1536. Sugar peas were also known at this time.

The common garden pea is an annual plant that has both bush and climbing varieties. It has bright green stems and foliage and white and purple flowers.

The pea is the small spherical seed contained within an elongated green pod. Generally catagorised as a vegetable, the pea is, in fact, a fruit and is high in protein and fibre.

The pea motif was used by the Elizabethan embroiderer in blackwork and coloured silk embroidery. It also became a favourite motif of the stumpwork embroiderers in the 17th century, who recreated the three-dimensional pods in delicate needlelace.

- -

Pease Pottage was a popular food in the winter and early spring when fresh food was scarce. Like a thick porridge, it was made from dried peas and often had pieces of salted bacon added for extra flavour.

Take two quarts of Pease, and put them into an Ordinary quantity of Water, and when they are almost boiled, take out a pint of the Pease whole, and strain all the rest. A little before you take out the pint of Pease, when they are all boiling together, put in almost an Ounce of Coriander-seed beaten very small, one Onion, some Mint, parsley, Winter-savoury, Sweet-Marjoram, all minced very small; when you have strained the Pease, put in the whole Pease and the strained again into the pot, and let them boil again, and a little before you take them up, put in half a pound of Sweet-butter. You must season them in due time, and in the ordinary proportion with Pepper and Salt.

English daisy

BELLIS PERENNIS

NATIVE to England, the English daisy is one of the most endearing wild plants and is thought by many to be the archetypal species of that name.

The name is thought to have come from its Anglo Saxon name 'deages eage', meaning day's eye as the flower opens in daylight and closes at night.

The English daisy is a small, low growing plant with spoon-shaped leaves and white-petalled flowers tipped with pink or red. Often referred to now as the 'lawn daisy', it naturalises in lawns and has an uncanny ability to avoid mower blades.

The daisy was dedicated to the goddesses of love, Aphrodite (Greek), Freya (Norse) or Venus (Roman). The Celts believed that daisies were the spirits of children who died at birth.

Medicinally, the daisy plant was used to treat liver ailments, fever and was applied externally to fresh wounds. Elizabethan herbalists used the acrid juice to treat gout and rheumatism and also recommended that it be 'sniffed up the nose' as a cure for migraine. Today, daisy oil is still used in homeopathic treatments.

Several double-flowering varieties had been introduced into the garden by the Elizabethan period and today the white and coloured cultivated varieties of *Bellis perennis* are valued as ornamentals. These are available in both single and double-flowered forms and create beautiful displays when grown with spring bulbs.

Pea & English Daisy

Wool

A = 1263 cream
B = 1311 med grape
C = A245 dk olive green
D = 1640 vy dk khaki green
E = 1652 olive green
F = 1692 med loden green
G = 1693 loden green
H = A472 vy lt autumn yellow
I = 1750 vy dk old gold
J = 1925 vy lt wood rose

Silk

A = 4102 cream
B = 1343 Parma violet
C = 2134 med grass green
D = 3736 dk khaki green
E = 2144 med grape green
F = 2115 med pistachio
G = 2114 pistachio
H = 2543 corn
I = 524 golden olive
J = 4621 ultra lt plum

THIS DESIGN USES

Detached chain • French knot • Outline stitch • Satin stitch
Satin stitch padding • Split stitch • Stem stitch

ORDER OF WORK

All embroidery is worked with one strand of thread.

Main stem

Using **D**, work the main stem in stem stitch, beginning at the right-hand pea leaf. Stitch along the stem, around the curving tip and back to the left-hand edge of the small pea pod.

English daisy

Stems

Stitch the stems to the flowers in stem stitch using **D**.

Leaves

Using **E**, outline each leaf with split stitch. Pad each side with straight stitch using the same colour. Work angled satin stitch over each leaf, beginning at the base on one side. Work up and around the tip and back to the base.

Flowers

Using **J**, stitch the first layer of petals in detached chain. Using **A**, stitch the second layer, offset to the first and positioning each stitch as shown (diag 1).

Work the third layer of detached chain in the same colour, again offsetting each stitch (diag 2).

Fill the centre of each flower with French knots using **H**.

Peas

Stems

Stitch the stems to the flowers and leaves in stem stitch using **F**. Using **C**, work the stems to the pea pods in outline stitch.

Leaves

Using **G**, outline each leaf with split stitch then fill the shape with rows of split stitch. Embroider the centre vein on each leaf in split stitch using **F**.

Flowers

Using **A**, outline the cream flower sections with split stitch. Fill with satin stitch padding and cover with satin stitch using the same colour (diag 3).

Outline the remaining petals in split stitch using **B**. Pad each shape with straight stitch and cover with satin stitch using the same colour. Using **C**, stitch the sepals with detached chain, working a small chain then a larger one around the first (diag 4).

Pods

Using **F** or **G**, outline each pod in split stitch. Fill each shape with satin stitch padding, working three circles of padding on the largest pod (diag 5). Cover with satin stitch using **F** or **G**. Using **C**, stitch the sepals in the same manner as the flowers.

Curlicues

Using **I**, stitch each curl using one row of stem stitch and one row of outline stitch for the wool and one row of outline or stem stitch for the silk.

ENGLISH DAISY

Layers of detached chain create a raised surface and allow a tiny hint of the base colour to show through.

Bring the thread to the front at the edge of the flower centre. Work a detached chain.

Work three more detached chain, positioning each one as shown.

Fill the areas between each stitch with chain, fanning them to fit the shape.

Change colour and bring the thread to the front between two stitches of the previous row.

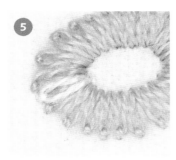

Work a detached chain, offsetting the stitch so that it sits over the edges of the stitches beneath.

Complete the second layer of stitches in this manner.

Work a third layer of stitches, again offsetting the stitches to those in the previous layer.

Fill the centre of the flower with French knots.

PEA MOTIF

THIS DESIGN USES

Detached chain • Outline stitch • Satin stitch
Satin stitch padding • Split stitch • Stem stitch

THREADS

Wool

A = 1263 cream
B = 1311 med grape
C = 1612 med hunter green
D = 1693 loden green
E = 1750 vy dk old gold

Silk

A = 4102 cream
B = 1343 Parma violet
C = 2134 med grass green
D = 2114 pistachio
E = 524 golden olive
F = 3736 dk khaki green

ORDER OF WORK

*All embroidery is worked with one strand
of thread.*

Stem

Using **E** for the wool and **F** for the silk,
work the stem in outline and/or stem
stitch. Work the stem to the right-hand
leaf in stem stitch using the same colour.
Using **C**, work the stems to the pea and
pea flower in outline stitch.

Flower

Using **A**, outline the upper petal in split
stitch. Fill with satin stitch padding and
cover with satin stitch using the same
colour. Using **B**, work the lower petal in
the same manner. Embroider the sepals in
satin stitch or detached chain using **C**.

Pod

Outline the pod in split stitch using **D**.
Fill with satin stitch padding and
cover with satin stitch using the
same colour. Stitch the sepals with
detached chain using **C**.

Leaves

Using **D**, outline the leaves in split stitch.
Fill each leaf with rows of split stitch in the
same colour. Embroider the veins in split
stitch using **C**.

ENGLISH DAISY MOTIF

THIS DESIGN USES

Detached chain • Outline stitch • Satin stitch
Satin stitch padding • Split stitch • Stem stitch • Straight stitch

THREADS

Wool

A = 1263 cream
B = 1652 olive green
C = A472 vy lt autumn yellow
D = 1750 vy dk old gold
E = 1925 vy lt wood rose

Silk

A = 4102 cream
B = 2144 med grape green
C = 2543 corn
D = 524 golden olive
E = 4621 ultra lt plum

ORDER OF WORK

All embroidery is worked with one strand of thread.

Stem

Using **D**, work the stem in outline and/or stem stitch. Work the stems to the flower and bud in stem stitch using **B**.

Flower and bud

Using **B**, outline the bud receptacle in split stitch. Fill with satin stitch padding and cover in satin stitch using the same thread. Work a layer of detached chain using **E** on the flower and bud. Using **A**, work a second and third layer, each time offsetting the stitches to the layer beneath. Fill the centre of the open flower with French knots using **C**.

Leaves

Outline the leaves in split stitch using **B**, pad with straight stitch and cover in satin stitch using the same colour.

Pear & Periwinkle

—— AFFECTION + FRIENDSHIP ——

Pear

PYRUS COMMUNIS

EVIDENCE of the existence of wild pears has been found at European sites dating back to 2500BC. Both Homer and Pliny mention pears in their writings around 300BC. The Romans brought plants to central Europe and used grafting techniques to produce high-yielding trees. These European pears were cultivated for centuries before they were hybridised with Chinese pears in the 19th century.

The pear is a deciduous medium-sized tree with glossy green leaves and white to pale pink blossom. The fruit is narrow at the top with a bulbous base and usually yellow in colour.

The pear was one of the fruit trees that the Elizabethans grew in their ornamental gardens. Consequently the pear tree and the pear both found their way into the embroiderer's imagination.

Elizabethan Pear Pie

- 1 quantity shortcrust pastry • 75ml white wine • 2 tbsp sugar
- pinch ground cloves • ¼ teaspoon cinnamon
- 3 large pears, peeled, halved and cored • 1 tbsp rosewater
- 1 tsp of melted butter • 1 additional tsp of rosewater
- 1–2 tbsp of brown sugar

Line a pie dish with pastry and blind bake at 200°C for 10 minutes. Reduce the temperature to 185°C and bake a further 5 minutes. Cool. Combine the wine, sugar, cloves and cinnamon in a heavy saucepan and bring to the boil. Add the pear halves and cook until the fruit is firm but easily pierced with a fork. Drain the fruit and reserve the syrup. Add 1 tbsp rosewater to the syrup and stir. Boil briskly until the syrup is thickened and reduced to ¼ cup. Cool. Coat the pear halves with syrup then place them in the pastry shell, flat side down and with the narrow ends towards the centre. Brush any extra syrup over the pears. Place the pastry lid over the pears. Combine the butter and extra tsp of rosewater. Brush over the pastry lid and sprinkle with the brown sugar. Bake at 200°C for 30 minutes or until the top is golden.

Periwinkle

VINCA MINOR

THE periwinkle is native to central and southern Europe. It has glossy, dark green leaves and blue-violet flowers with five petals. It spreads along the ground, sending out new roots along the stems and can be very difficult to eradicate.

The plant has been used in medicine for centuries and the Latin name, *Vinca*, is derived from *vincere*, meaning 'to overcome'.

European herbalists have used periwinkle for headaches, vertigo and poor memory since mediaeval times.

Periwinkle is also the name of a snail-like mollusc that was greatly esteemed by the Elizabethans.

Carrying periwinkles was believed to increase prosperity and keep away dangerous beasts, poisonous snakes, terror and evil spirits, while gazing upon the flowers was thought to restore lost memories. Periwinkles became symbols of immortality and the love between a husband and wife and were often used to fashion 'chaplets' or circlets of flowers that were worn around the head.

Pear & Periwinkle

THIS DESIGN USES

Fly stitch • French knot • Long and short stitch • Outline stitch
Satin stitch • Satin stitch padding • Split stitch • Stem stitch
Straight stitch

THREADS

Wool

A = 1263 cream
B = A101 vy lt purple
C = 1560 dk glacier
D = A745 med bright China blue
E = A244 med olive green
F = 1643 khaki green
G = 1691 dk loden green
H = 1692 med loden green
I = 1694 lt loden green
J = 1695 vy lt loden green
K = A472 vy lt autumn yellow
L = 1730 vy dk honey gold
M = 1733 honey gold
N = 1750 vy dk old gold
O = 1920 vy dk wood rose

Silk

A = 4102 cream
B = 1342 lt Parma violet
C = 4914 med hyacinth
D = 1422 lt marine blue
E = 3735 med khaki green
F = 3733 lt khaki green
G = 2126 dk parrot green
H = 2115 med pistachio
I = 2132 lt grass green
J = 2131 vy lt grass green
K = 2543 corn
L = 2246 vy dk colonial gold
M = 2515 med copper yellow
N = 524 golden olive
O = 4625 med plum

ORDER OF WORK

All embroidery is worked with one strand of thread.

Main stem

Using **O**, work the main stem in stem stitch, beginning at the upper right-hand edge of the large pear. Stitch down along the stem, around the curving tip and back to the petal of the side-view periwinkle flower.

Pear

Stems

Stitch the stems to the left-hand pair of leaves in stem stitch using **O**.

Leaves

Using **F**, outline each leaf with split stitch. Fill each leaf with rows of split stitch in the same colour. Using **E**, stitch the leaf veins and stems in split stitch or outline stitch.

Flower

Using **A**, outline the petals in split stitch. Fill with satin stitch padding and cover with satin stitch in the same colour. Work French knots above the petal tips using **K**. Outline the receptacle in split stitch and cover in satin stitch using **F**. Using **E**, work two straight stitches over the satin stitch as indicated (diag 1).

Embroider the flower stem in stem stitch using **E**.

Fruit

Outline the pears in split stitch using **M** for the large pear and **K** for the smaller fruit. Using the photograph as a guide to colour placement, stitch the large pear in long and short stitch using **K**, **M** and **N**. Work a line of outline stitch around the lower half of the pear using **L**. Work outline stitch for the stem and straight stitches at the top of the fruit in the same colour.

Stitch the smaller pear in long and short stitch using **M**, **K**, **I** and **J**. Work a line of outline stitch under the base of the pear using **N**. Work outline stitch for the stem and straight stitches at the base and neck of the fruit using the same colour.

Periwinkle

Stems

Using **O**, embroider the stems to the leaves in stem stitch.

Leaves

Using **G** or **H**, outline each leaf in split stitch and cover in satin stitch using the same colour.

Flowers and buds

Using **D**, outline the open flowers and side-view flower in split stitch and pad the side-view flower petals in satin stitch padding. Cover all the petals with satin stitch. Embroider a fly stitch around the outer edge of the petals of the open flowers using **C**. Work straight stitch highlights over the base of each petal on the open flowers using **B**. Using **A**, fill the centre of each flower with intersecting straight stitches. Stitch a French knot at the centre using **D**. Work the buds in satin stitch using **C**, **G** and **H**. Stitch the bud stems in stem stitch using **G**.

Curlicues

Using **N**, stitch each curl using one row of stem stitch and one row of outline stitch for the wool and one row of outline or stem stitch for the silk.

CURLICUES

A line of outline stitch and a parallel line of stem will create wheat stitch, similar in appearance to chain stitch.

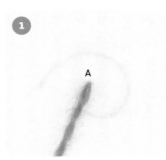

Bring the thread to the front at A.

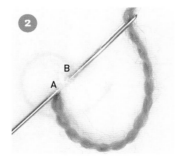

Take the needle to the back at B and emerge at A. Ensure that the thread is below the needle.

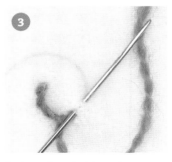

Reduce the stitch length to go around the tight curl.

Continue working stem stitch along the line. Take the thread to the back at the end of the row.

Wrong side. On the back of the work, hook the thread through the back of a stitch.

Bring the thread to the front at the end of the line.

Work back along the curl in outline stitch, matching the length of the stitches to the first row.

PERIWINKLE MOTIF

THIS DESIGN USES

French knot • Fly stitch • Outline stitch • Satin stitch
Split stitch • Stem stitch • Straight stitch

THREADS

Wool

A = 1263 cream
B = A101 vy lt purple
C = 1560 dk glacier
D = A745 med bright China blue
E = 1694 lt loden green
F = 1750 vy dk old gold

Silk

A = 4102 cream
B = 1342 lt Parma violet
C = 4914 med hyacinth
D = 1422 lt marine blue
E = 2132 lt grass green
F = 4625 med plum

ORDER OF WORK

All embroidery is worked with one strand of thread.

Stem

Using **F**, work the stem in outline and/or stem stitch. Work the stem to the leaf in stem stitch using the same colour.

Flower

Using **D**, outline the flower in split stitch. Stitch the petals in satin stitch using the same colour. Embroider a fly stitch around the outer edge of each petal using **C**. Work several straight stitches into the base of each petal using **B**. Using **A**, fill the centre with intersecting straight stitches. Stitch a French knot at the centre of the flower using **C**.

Leaf

Outline the leaf in split stitch using **E**, then cover in satin stitch using the same colour.

Plum &
Cinquefoil

—— INDEPENDENCE + COURAGE ——

Plum

PRUNUS DOMESTICA

THE common European plum is thought to have originated around the Caucasus and from early writings, the species is at least 2,000 years old. The fruit grows on a small tree that produces groups of showy flowers in the spring. When ripe, the fruit skin and pulp varies in colour from rich dark purple to pale cream. The plum is a soft fruit that bruises easily but contains a high percentage of juice.

Plums can be eaten when ripe, or dried and stored as prunes. The Elizabethans were fond of fruit wines and the plum was another suitable variety for this use.

The entry in Gerard's Herball or General Historie of Plantes 1633 reads:

"Prunus Domestica. Of the Plum tree. Plummes that be ripe and new gathered from the tree, what sort soeuer they are of, do moisten and coole, and yeeld unto the body very little nourishment, and the same nothing good at all: for as Plummes do very quickly rot, so is also the iuice of them apt to putrifie in the body, and likewise to cause the meat to putrifie which is taken with them... Dried Plums, commonly called Prunes, are wholsomer, and more pleasant to the stomack, they teeld more nonrishment, and better, and such as cannot easily putrifie..."

To make Paste of Plumbs

Take your Plumbs, and put them into a Pot, cover them close, and set them into a Pot of seething Water, and so let them be till they be tender, then pour forth their Liquor, and strain the Pulp through a Canvas strainer, then take to half a Pound of the Pulp of Plumbs half a Pound of the Pulp of Pippins, beat them together, and take their weight in fine Sugar, with as much Water as will wet it, and boil it to a Candy height; then put in your Pulp, and boil them together till it will come from the bottom of the Posnet, then dust your Plates with searced Sugar, and so keep them in a Stove to dry.

Cinquefoil

POTENTILLA VERNA

LIKE strawberries, the cinquefoil belongs to the rose family. Most plants in this species look similar to the strawberry in leaf and flower form but have inedible fruit.

The name 'cinquefoil' comes from Middle English and means 'five leaf'. This is another English wildflower that inhabited fields, roadsides and open woods. It spreads by producing runners that then root from spaced nodes or joints. One botanist commented that the cinquefoil "...weaves its embroidery over the stony and barren roadside."

It can also reproduce from seed. The flowers are most commonly yellow but some varieties have orange or red blooms. The simple, five-petalled flower is a very common heraldry symbol and can be found on coats of arms throughout England and France. It served as a motif for a man who had achieved 'mastery over the self' and could only be used by those, it was deemed, had done so.

The cinquefoil has been used in medicine for centuries as a herbal astringent and to stop bleeding, and was one of the plants that was believed by the Elizabethans to have value in curing those suffering from 'demon-induced' illness.

In botany the term 'cinquefoil' evokes a large number of plants in the Rosaceae family, including buttercups and potentilla, but in heraldry it signifies a five-petal flower and was a popular architectural motif when ornamenting buildings.

THREADS

Wool

A = 1263 cream
B = 1311 med grape
C = A101 vy lt purple
D = A121 ultra lt terracotta
E = 1611 dk hunter green
F = 1690 vy dk loden green
G = 1692 med loden green
H = 1693 loden green
I = 1726 vy lt autumn yellow
J = 1730 vy dk honey gold
K = 1750 vy dk old gold
L = 1920 vy dk wood rose
M = 1925 vy lt wood rose
N = 1940 vy dk cranberry

Silk

A = 4102 cream
B = 1343 Parma violet
C = 1342 lt Parma violet
D = 4643 lt raisin
E = 2135 dk grass green
F = 2116 dk pistachio
G = 2115 med pistachio
H = 2114 pistachio
I = 2514 copper yellow
J = 2246 vy dk colonial gold
K = 524 golden olive
L = 4625 med plum
M = 4621 ultra lt plum
N = 1026 vy dk rose

Plum & Cinquefoil

THIS DESIGN USES

French knot • Long and short stitch • Outline stitch • Satin stitch
Satin stitch padding • Split stitch • Stem stitch • Straight stitch

ORDER OF WORK

All embroidery is worked with one strand of thread.

Main stem

Using **J**, work the main stem in stem stitch, beginning at the left-hand plum. Stitch down the stem, around the curving tip and back to the starting point.

Plum

Stems

Stitch the stems to the plums and flowers in stem stitch using **J**.

Leaves

Using **F**, outline each large leaf with split stitch then cover in satin stitch using the same colour. Using **G**, stitch the small leaf in the same manner.

Flowers and buds

Using **A**, outline the petals in split stitch. Fill with satin stitch padding and cover with satin stitch in the same colour. Using **M**, work straight stitch highlights over the base of each petal of the large flower. Fill the centre with satin stitch using **H**. Work a ring of French knots around the centre in the same colour. Stitch the sepals on the side-view flowers in straight stitch using **E** or **G**. Embroider the sepals over the bud in a similar manner with **E** and **G**.

Fruit

Outline each plum in split stitch using **B**. Using the photograph as a guide to colour placement, stitch the plums in long and short stitch using **B**, **C** and **D**. Work a line of split stitch down the centre of the large plums using **D**. Repeat for the smaller plum using **B**.

Cinquefoil

Stems

Stitch the stems to the flowers in stem stitch using **G** and **H**.

Leaves

Using **G**, outline the large leaves in split stitch and cover with satin stitch using the same colour. Embroider the small leaves in satin stitch using **H**.

Flowers and buds

Outline the petals of the large flower and two side view flowers in split stitch using **N**.

Using the photograph as a guide to colour placement, stitch the petals in satin stitch using **L** or **N**. Using **L**, work straight stitches over the base of the petals on the large flower and left-hand side flower. Work a partial line of stem stitch beneath the front petals using **L**. Using **H**, stitch the centre of the large flower in satin stitch. Work a ring of French knots around the centre and scatter knots at the base of the petals using **I**. Fill the small bud above the large flower in satin stitch using **L**. Stitch the sepals in straight stitch using **H** for the small bud and **G** for the other flowers.

Curlicues

Using **K**, embroider each curl using one row of stem stitch and one row of outline stitch for the wool and one row of outline or stem stitch for the silk.

SATIN STITCH LEAF

Work the split stitch outline carefully as this will help ensure that the edge of the leaf is smooth.

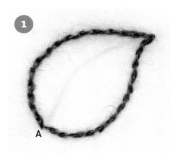

Bring the thread to the front at A. Work a split stitch outline around the leaf.

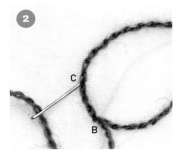

Bring the thread to the front at B. Take the needle to the back at C.

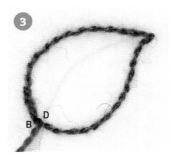

Pull the thread through. Bring the thread to the front at D, just above B.

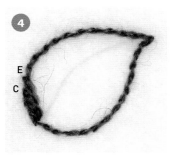

Take the needle to the back at E, just above C.

Continue working in this manner to just below the leaf tip.

Fan the stitches around the tip, using the same hole at the centre vein.

Work the remaining side in satin stitch taking care to maintain the correct angle.

CINQUEFOIL MOTIF

THIS DESIGN USES
French knot • Satin stitch • Stem stitch • Split stitch
Straight stitch

THREADS

Wool

A = 1940 vy dk cranberry
B = 1693 loden green
C = 1690 vy dk loden green
D = 1730 vy dk honey gold
E = 1726 vy lt autumn yellow
F = 1920 vy dk wood rose

Silk

A = 1026 vy dk rose
B = 2114 pistachio
C = 2116 dk pistachio
D = 2246 vy dk colonial gold
E = 2514 copper yellow
F = 4625 med plum

ORDER OF WORK

All embroidery is worked with one strand of thread.

Stem

Stitch the stem to the flower and leaf with stem stitch using **D**.

Leaf

Outline the leaf with split stitch and cover each half with angled satin stitch using **C**.

Flower

Outline each petal with split stitch and cover with satin stitch using **A**. Work straight stitches over the base of each petal using **F** and outline the outer edge of the lower two petals with stem stitch using the same thread.

Fill the flower centre with satin stitch using **B**. Work a ring of French knots around the centre and scatter knots at the base of the petals using **E**.

Stitch Glossary

Blanket stitch

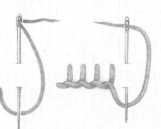

Bullion knot

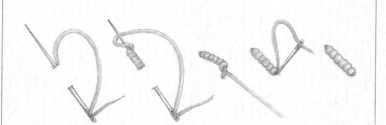

Coral stitch

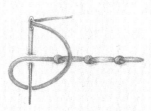

Corded Coral stitch

Couching

A laid thread is attached using a second thread.

Detached chain

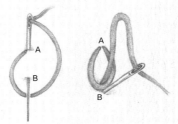

Fly stitch

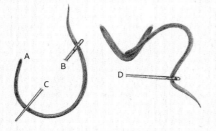

French knot

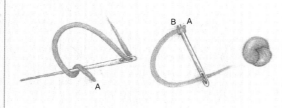

Long and short blanket stitch

Long and short stitch

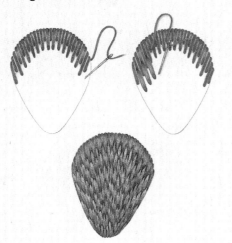

Satin stitch

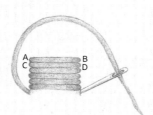

Split stitch

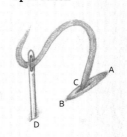

Up and down blanket stitch

Straight stitch

Whipping

Kits

PINWHEEL KITS

Each *Flowers for Elizabeth* pinwheel kit contains enough threads to stitch your selected motif
onto a pinwheel, scissor sheath and needlebook.

Borage & Honeysuckle

*Blue borage and golden
honeysuckle*

Poppy & Columbine

*Bright red field poppy and
purple columbine*

Raspberry & Tulip

*Raspberries, blossoms and
purple tulips*

Primrose & Thistle

*Soft yellow primroses and
purple thistles*

Acorn & Gillyflower

*Gleaming acorns with pink
and white gillyflowers*

Heartsease & Eglantine

*Violet and gold heartsease
with pink eglantine and
red hips*

Cornflower & Strawberry

*Blue cornflowers paired
with luscious red berries and
white blossoms*

Pomegranate & Cranesbill

*Red fruits beneath
delicate blue flowers and
green seed pods*

Peony & Buttercup

*Stunning peony and golden
yellow buttercup*

Pea & English Daisy

*Pea pods, pea flowers and
white daisies*

Pear & Periwinkle

*Ripe, golden pears and
delicate periwinkle*

Plum & Cinquefoil

*Purple pears, white blossoms
and vibrant cinquefoil*

NEEDLEWORK ACCESSORIES KITS

Use the threads from the pinwheel kits to complete your chosen motif.

SCISSOR SHEATH KIT

The curved upper edge and sprinkle of paillettes adds regal elegance to this silk sheath for your most treasured needlework scissors.

NEEDLEBOOK KIT

The silk needlebook contains wool flannel pages and handy pockets for needle packets.

BLANKET KITS

Blanket Kit includes fabrics, sewing thread, embroidery threads and needles.

Thread Pack Kit containing embroidery threads also available.

Decorative blanket featuring an embellished lattice of wool and cashmere velour showcasing beloved flowers and fruits from Elizabethan gardens, each worked in wool threads. The twelve main designs feature paired motifs on curling stems. A further twelve individual designs decorate the edges surrounding the main motifs.

Inspirations Ready-to-Stitch kits available at:

inspirationsstudios.com

Construction & Embroidery Designs

THE PINWHEEL

All seam allowances are 1cm (⅜"). The shaded areas on the following diagrams indicate the right side of the fabric.

1. Preparing the embroidery

Remove the embroidery from the hoop and, if required, press face down on a well-padded surface. Remove any remaining heat-soluble marker.

Cut two 8cm (3⅛") diameter circles of card.

> **HINT:** Use an 8cm (3⅛") diameter glass to mark the circles.

If desired, sand the cut edges gently to ensure that they are smooth. Cut two 10cm (4") diameter circles and two 6cm (2½") diameter circles of thin fusible wadding.

2. Preparing the front and back

Leaving a tail at each end, work a line of running stitch around each large wadding circle, 1cm (⅜") from the edge (diag 1).

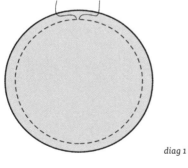

diag 1

Position one small circle of wadding at the centre of each card disc and fuse in place with a warm iron. Place each disc, wadding side down, onto a large circle of wadding. Pull the thread tails to gather the wadding around the disc and tie off firmly (diag 2).

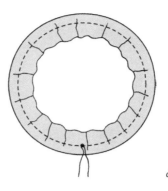

diag 2

On the embroidered fabrics measure out 1cm (⅜") from the running stitch circle and mark (diag 3).

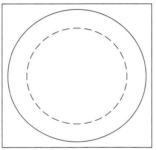

diag 3

Cut out the fabric along the outer marked line.

Leaving a tail at each end, work a line of running stitch around each fabric circle 5mm (³⁄₁₆") from the fabric edge.

Centre a prepared disc onto the back of each fabric circle, aligning the edge of the disc with the marked circle outline. Pull up the threads and tie off firmly. Working around the circle, lace the fabric using strong thread (diag 4).

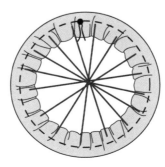

diag 4

Remove the tacking. Press the back of each disc to flatten the gathered fabric.

3. Joining the front and back

With wrong sides facing and matching edges, place the discs together, ensuring that the designs are correctly oriented. Stitch the discs together with coral stitch using two strands of *Soie d'Alger* 524 and placing the stitches approximately 3mm (⅛") apart.

4. Finishing

Between every second coral stitch push a glass-head pin into the pinwheel (diag 5).

diag 5

THE SCISSOR SHEATH

All seam allowances are 1cm (⅜"). The shaded areas on the following diagrams indicate the right side of the fabric.

To obtain the most accurate results, cut one back and one front from the thin card. Use these pieces as templates for cutting the fabric.

CUTTING LAYOUT

1. Sheath front
2. Sheath back and lining
3. Sheath front lining

1. Preparing the card, wadding and fabric

Position the front card over the back of the embroidered piece and check the shaping on the fabric (diag 1).

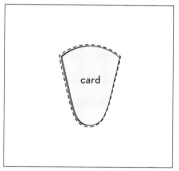

diag 1

Adjust the shaping if necessary. Using the front and back card pieces as templates, mark the shaping for one sheath front lining and two sheath backs onto the right side of the silk fabric ensuring that there is 2cm (¾") between each piece. Work running stitch around the marked shaping using matching sewing thread. Leaving a 1cm (⅜") seam allowance around

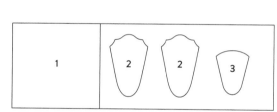

Cutting layout

each piece, cut out. Carefully finger press the seam allowance to the right side of the fabric, clipping where necessary, and tack in place on each piece (diag 2).

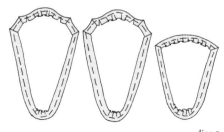

diag 2

Do not press.

Using the card templates cut one front and two back pieces from the wadding. Using a warm iron fuse the wadding to one side of the front card and both sides of the back card.

2. Preparing the sheath front

Using the lacing thread and leaving a 5cm (2") tail at each end, work a line of gathering 6mm (¼") out from the running stitch outline on the embroidered fabric (diag 3).

diag 3

Cut out the embroidered piece leaving a 1cm (⅜") seam allowance from the line of tacking. Position the front sheath card, wadding side down, over the back of the embroidery. Draw up the lacing thread tails firmly and tie off (diag 4).

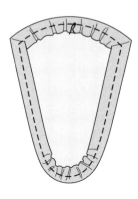

diag 4

Adjust the gathers so that the fabric is smooth.

With wrong sides together and matching raw edges position the front lining piece over the back of the card. Overcast the folded edges of the fabrics together around the edge using matching sewing thread (diag 5).

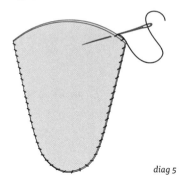

diag 5

3. Preparing the sheath back

Position one piece of prepared silk on each side of the padded back card. Hold in place with pins or clips. Using the silk sewing thread and beginning at one side of the centre top, overcast the edges of the fabrics together (diag 6).

diag 6

SCISSOR SHEATH / CONTINUED

4. Joining the front and back

Cut a 50cm (20") length of seven strands of *Soie d'Alger* 524 for the cording. Take the cording thread through the back of the sheath front and emerge at the top right-hand edge. Using three strands of *Soie d'Alger* 524, and beginning at the right-hand side, work corded coral stitch across the top edge of the sheath front only. Leave the threads hanging. Position the sheath front over the back and overcast the pieces together through the edges using the silk sewing thread (diag 7).

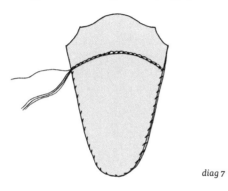

diag 7

Using the left threads work corded coral stitch around the outer edge of the sheath (diag 8).

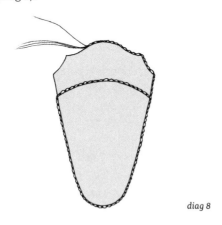

diag 8

THE NEEDLEBOOK

Cutting Out

Where pattern pieces are not provided, cut the pieces according to the measurements below.

IVORY SILK DUCHESS SATIN

Needlebook front: cut one 20cm (8") square

Needlebook back: cut one 12.5cm x 11cm wide (5" x 4⅜")

Needlebook front and back lining: cut two, 12cm x 10.5cm wide (4¾" x 4⅛")

Needlebook pocket: cut two, each 7cm x 10.5cm wide (2¾" x 4⅛")

Needlebook spine: Cut one 11cm x 3cm wide (4⅜" x 1⅛")

WADDING

Needlebook front and back: Cut two, each 10cm x 8.5cm wide (4" x 3⅜")

Cut two 12.5cm x 11cm wide (5" x 4⅜")

CARD

Needlebook front and back: Cut four, each 10cm x 8.5cm wide (4" x 3⅜")

WOOL FLANNEL

(cut with the pinking shears)

Needlebook pages: cut two, each 9.5cm x 17cm wide (3¾" x 6¾")

CUTTING LAYOUT

Ivory duchess silk satin

1. Needlebook front
2. Needlebook back
3. Needlebook front and back lining
4. Needlebook pocket (2)
5. Needlebook spine

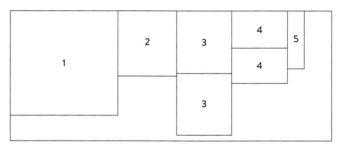

Cutting layout

Construction

All seam allowances are 1cm (⅜") unless specified. The shaded areas on the following diagrams indicate the right side of the fabric.

1. Preparing the embroidery

Remove the embroidery from the hoop and, if required, press face down on a well-padded surface. Remove any remaining heat-soluble marker.

Cut the required pieces of card and, if desired, sand the cut edges gently to ensure that they are smooth.

2. Preparing the card, wadding and fabric

Glue two pieces of card together for each side of the cover. Using a warm iron fuse one small rectangle of wadding onto one side of the card. Centre the card, wadding side down onto one large piece of wadding. Lace the large piece over the card (diag 1).

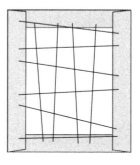

diag 1

Press.

Repeat for the remaining piece.

Leaving a 1.5cm (⅝") border outside the tacked line cut out the embroidered fabric. Centre one padded card over the back of the embroidery, fold over the seam allowance and lace the fabric over the card.

Lace the piece of silk for the needlebook back over the second piece of padded card in the same manner.

3. Preparing and attaching the lining

On one long edge of each pocket piece turn under 5mm (³⁄₁₆") twice and slip stitch in place with the silk sewing thread (diag 2).

diag 2

Press.

Position each pocket, with the hemmed edge uppermost, over a lining piece. Tack around the fabrics 1cm (⅜") from the raw edges. This will hold the fabrics together and mark the position to turn under the fabric. Carefully finger press the seam allowance to the back of the fabric and tack in place on each piece (diag 3).

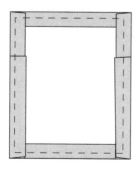

diag 3

Do not press. With wrong sides together and matching folded edges position each lining piece over a cover. Overcast the folded edges of the fabrics together around the edge using the silk sewing thread.

4. Preparing and attaching the spine

Fold under 5mm (³⁄₁₆") on both short ends of the spine strip and tack in place.

Turn under 5mm (³⁄₁₆") on one long edge and tack in place. Turn under 7mm (⁵⁄₁₆") on the second long edge and tack in place. Turn under a second 5mm (³⁄₁₆") on the first long edge and slip stitch in place down the centre of the strip (diag 4).

Using the silk sewing thread, overcast the spine to the back and front covers through the fabric folds.

Beginning at the lower left-hand corner of the front cover and using seven strands of *Soie d'Alger* 524 for the cording and three strands of *Soie d'Alger* 524 for the coral stitch, work corded coral stitch around three sides of the front cover, working across the lower edge up the right-hand side and across the upper edge.

Work corded coral stitch across the upper short edge of the spine and down the seam joining the back cover to the spine (diag 5).

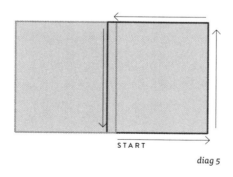

START

diag 5

End off the threads. Beginning at the upper right-hand corner of the back cover work corded coral stitch around the remaining three sides, across the lower short edge of the spine and up the seam between the front cover and the spine (diag 6).

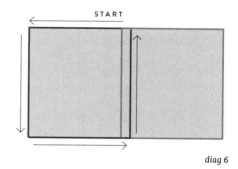

START

diag 6

5. Pages

Layer the rectangles of wool flannel over one another and tack down the centre (diag 7).

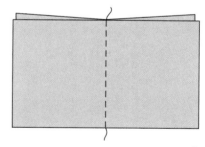

diag 7

Stitch the pages to the centre of the spine along the tacked line, taking care not to go through all layers of the spine.

Remove the tacking.

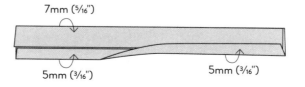

7mm (⁵⁄₁₆")

5mm (³⁄₁₆") 5mm (³⁄₁₆")

diag 4

NEEDLEBOOK / CONTINUED

6. Finishing

Leaving a 10cm (4") tail at the base, tie one strand of *Soie d'Alger* 524 onto the pebble bead. Wrap the pebble bead with thread, taking the needle down through the centre hole, until it is completely covered. Take the needle down through the centre hole, catching the wrapping threads to secure and trim away the excess thread, leaving a 10cm (4") tail at the base. Using the two thread tails, stitch the covered bead in place at the centre of the edge of the back cover. Using two strands of the same thread work an up and down blanket stitch loop to fit the bead at the centre of the edge of the front cover (diag 8).

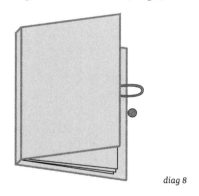

diag 8

Remove any visible running stitch and fabric marker.

THE BLANKET

1. Preparing the fabric and backing

Remove any remaining tacking and design lines. Press the embroidery, face down on a well-padded surface.

Lay the twill fabric, with the wrong side uppermost, onto a large, flat surface. Position the blanket with the right side uppermost over the twill, aligning all raw edges. Pin the layers together, ensuring they are smooth. Working outwards from the centre, tack the layers together in a grid (diag 1).

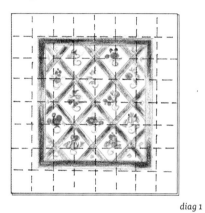

diag 1

Tack around the fabrics, 2.5cm (1") in from the raw edges.

2. Attaching the binding

Using the template on page 147, cut the shaping for the corner mitres at each end of the 15cm (6") binding strips of black velour. With right sides together and matching raw edges, pin the binding strips together. Beginning and ending 1cm (⅜") from the raw edges, stitch the corner seams, ensuring that the two short strips are on opposite sides to one another (diag 2).

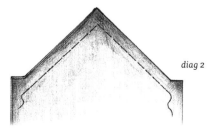

diag 2

Trim. Turn the binding to the right side and gently press (diag 3).

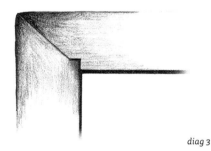

diag 3

With right sides together and matching raw edges, pin one shorter edge of the binding along one short side of the blanket, beginning and ending 1cm (⅜") from the raw edge (diag 4).

1cm
(⅜")

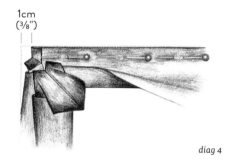

diag 4

Stitch. Repeat for the remaining three sides. Fold under 1cm (⅜") on the remaining raw edges and tack in place. Fold the binding to the back. Aligning the folded edges with the previous stitchline, pin and handstitch in place.

3. Finishing

At the intersection of each lattice strip, bring two strands of *Colonial Persian Yarn* 1220 to the front under the central French knot, leaving a 10cm (4") tail at the back. Make a small stitch and take the needle to the back through both layers. Tie the ends with a firm double knot. Trim the threads to 2.5cm (1"). Press gently.

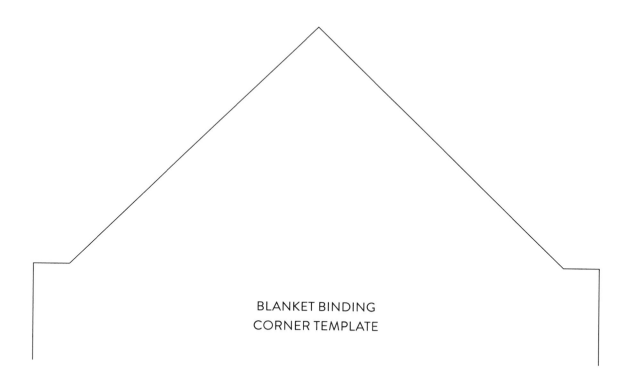

BLANKET BINDING
CORNER TEMPLATE

NEEDLEBOOK
FRONT SHAPING
AND CARD TEMPLATE

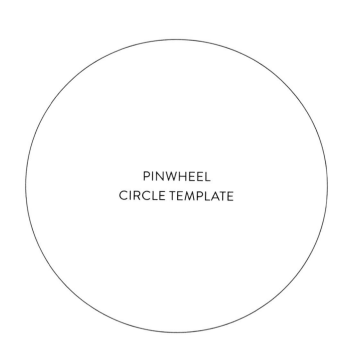

PINWHEEL
CIRCLE TEMPLATE

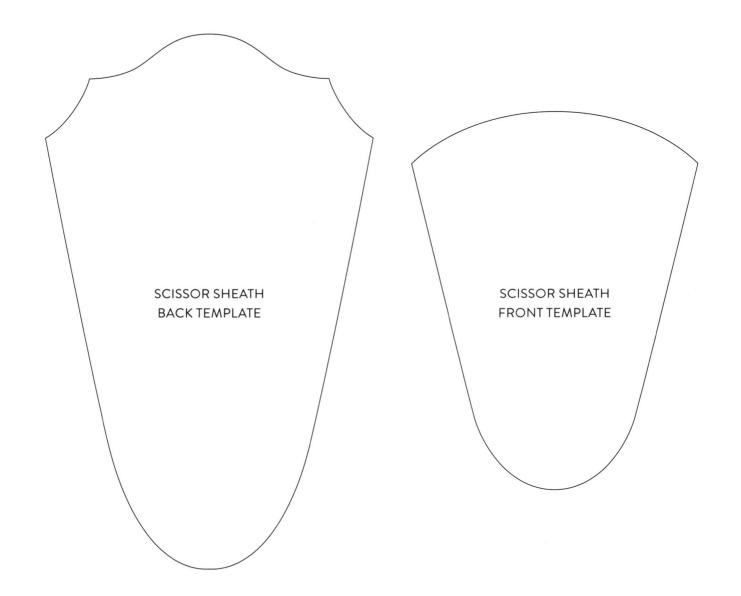

SCISSOR SHEATH
BACK TEMPLATE

SCISSOR SHEATH
FRONT TEMPLATE

PLACEMENT
GUIDE

PLACEMENT
GUIDE

BORAGE &
HONEYSUCKLE

page 30

PLACEMENT
GUIDE

PLACEMENT
GUIDE

POPPY &
COLUMBINE

page 38

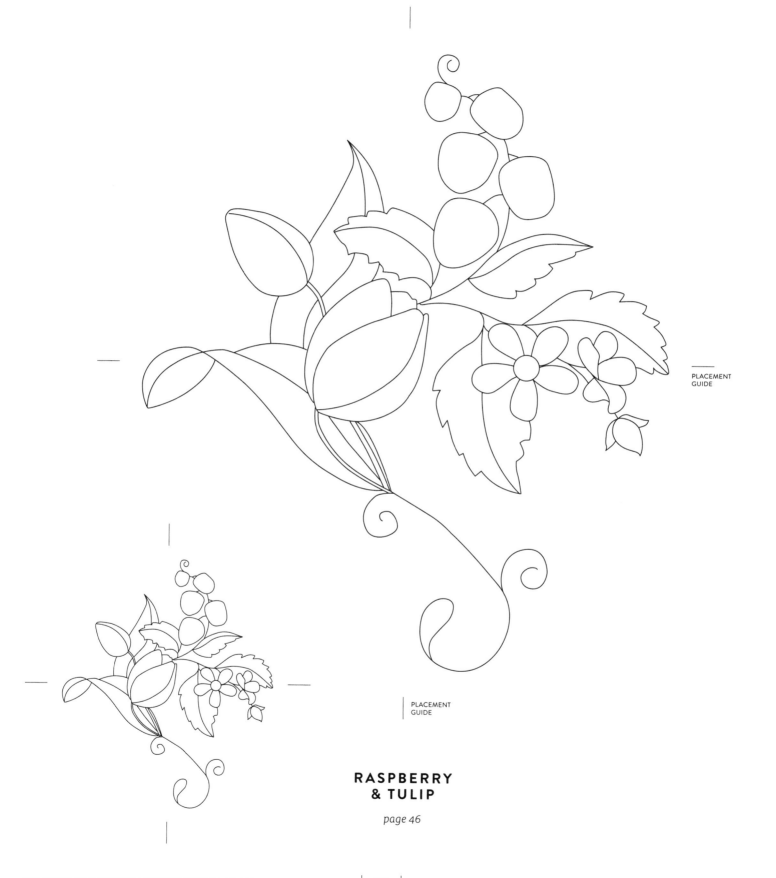

PLACEMENT
GUIDE

PLACEMENT
GUIDE

RASPBERRY
& TULIP

page 46

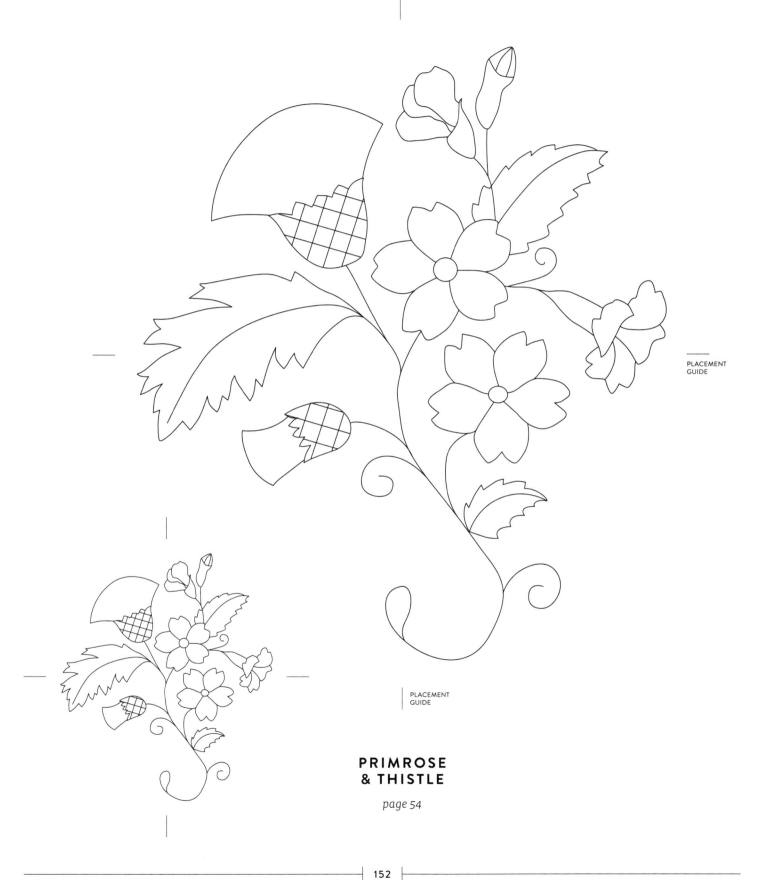

PLACEMENT
GUIDE

PLACEMENT
GUIDE

PRIMROSE
& THISTLE

page 54

PLACEMENT
GUIDE

PLACEMENT
GUIDE

ACORN &
GILLYFLOWER

page 62

PLACEMENT
GUIDE

PLACEMENT
GUIDE

HEARTSEASE
& EGLANTINE

page 72

PLACEMENT
GUIDE

PLACEMENT
GUIDE

CORNFLOWER
& STRAWBERRY

page 82

PLACEMENT
GUIDE

PLACEMENT
GUIDE

POMEGRANATE
& CRANESBILL

page 92

PLACEMENT
GUIDE

PLACEMENT
GUIDE

PEONY &
BUTTERCUP

page 100

PLACEMENT
GUIDE

PLACEMENT
GUIDE

PEA &
ENGLISH DAISY

page 110

PLACEMENT
GUIDE

PLACEMENT
GUIDE

PEAR &
PERIWINKLE

page 120

PLACEMENT
GUIDE

PLACEMENT
GUIDE

PLUM & CINQUEFOIL

page 128

HONEYSUCKLE MOTIF

page 37

POPPY MOTIF

page 45

PRIMROSE MOTIF

page 61

RASPBERRY MOTIF

page 53

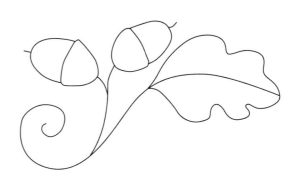

ACORN MOTIF

page 69

GILLYFLOWER MOTIF

page 70

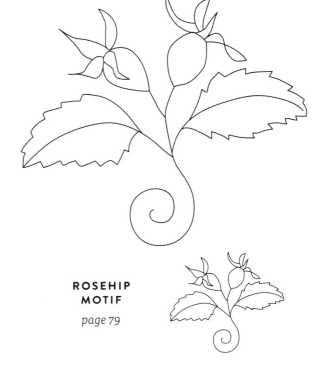

ROSEHIP MOTIF

page 79

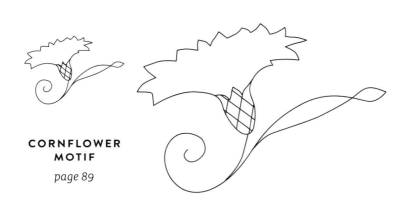

CORNFLOWER MOTIF

page 89

HEARTSEASE MOTIF

page 80

STRAWBERRY MOTIF

page 90

CRANESBILL MOTIF

page 99

PEA MOTIF

page 117

PEONY MOTIF

page 107

BUTTERCUP MOTIF

page 108

ENGLISH DAISY MOTIF

page 118

**PERIWINKLE
MOTIF**

page 127

**CINQUEFOIL
MOTIF**

page 135